Succession in Asian Family Firms

Succession in Asian Family Firms

Shaheena Janjuha-Jivraj

338.6
J 33ʌ

First published 2006 by
PALGRAVE MACMILLAN
Houndmills, Basingstoke, Hampshire RG21 6XS and
175 Fifth Avenue, New York, N.Y. 10010
Companies and representatives throughout the world

PALGRAVE MACMILLAN is the global academic imprint of the Palgrave
Macmillan division of St. Martin's Press, LLC and of Palgrave Macmillan Ltd.
Macmillan® is a registered trademark in the United States, United Kingdom
and other countries. Palgrave is a registered trademark in the European
Union and other countries.

ISBN-13: 978–1–4039–4301–9 hardback
ISBN-10: 1–4039–4301–X hardback

This book is printed on paper suitable for recycling and made from fully
managed and sustained forest sources.

A catalogue record for this book is available from the British Library.

Library of Congress Cataloging-in-Publication Data
Janjuha-Jivraj, Shaheena, 1972–
    Succession in Asian family firms / Shaheena Janjuha-Jivraj.
       p.   cm.
    Includes bibliographical references and index.
    ISBN 1–4039–4301–X (cloth)
    1. Family-owned business enterprises—Asia.   2. Business enterprises,
    Foreign.   I. Title.
    HD62.25.J36 2005
    338.6—dc22   2005049325

10   9   8   7   6   5   4   3   2   1
15   14   13   12   11   10   09   08   07   06

Printed and bound in Great Britain by
Antony Rowe Ltd, Chippenham and Eastbourne

To Sorain and Amina Janjuha

Contents

List of Tables and Figures

Tables

Figures

Acknowledgments

There are many organisations and individuals who have supported the research and have had an invaluable role in production of this book. I am very grateful for their commitment, time and generosity. First a big thank you to the family firms who agreed to participate in the research and allowed me into their world with such openness and enthusiasm. I am also grateful to various individuals who provided introductions to contacts and family businesses in Kenya, the United States and the United Kingdom.

Many thanks to colleagues who provided advice and feedback on the ideas during development of this research, particular thanks to Keith Dickson and Adrian Woods.

The support of family and friends has been invaluable during this process; although there are many people to thank, I am particularly grateful for the generosity offered by the Amermans, Verjees and Mirzas.

I am indebted to my family for their support during the research and the writing up of this book.

1
Family Firms in the South Asian Diaspora

Family business research is a fast-growing field of interest for academics and practitioners as well as the business community. Business start-up is invariably supported by the social capital of the individual. This resource is usually drawn from family and wider kinship members of the entrepreneur. The growth and survival of small firms has been a constant area of debate, particularly as economies have encouraged a greater enterprising culture since the 1970s. The field of entrepreneurship and small firms has gradually become an important field of research in Management and Business, albeit at differing rates across the globe. The growth of businesses can be unpredictable and family labour often provides a critical buffer to help businesses survive these turbulent periods. The natural progression from entrepreneurship and business start-up is to consider what happens after these businesses have achieved growth and have to face succession?

Family businesses are the most complex form of organisation, the interaction of the logical business form with the emotional family unit generates situations of intense emotion and conflicting loyalties. Family involvement in a business can create a source of enormous benefit and advantage for the business (for example deferred gratification, loyalty, shared goals, trustworthiness), however when problems arise their damage can not only destroy the business, but also the family and have a wider ripple effect on the business and personal communities of all those involved.

Emotional, traumatic, divisive, challenging – these are some of the words often used to describe succession within family firms. This is supported by the statistics often quoted relating to the survival of the first-second generation and second-third generation. Since the 1970s various researchers have tried to explore and further understand the dynamics of family relations during the period of generation transfer, however the foundation of this research is predominantly within Western family firms. Much of this work, however, emphasises the importance of the owner *within* the business and the family involved in an ad hoc manner. The cultural traits and values that have influenced a considerable part of family research do not coincide with the system evident in first-generation South Asian firms. Research on South Asian firms in the West has been somewhat limited and often presented within the context of the Western firms. The basis of this research lies in the assumption that family values and traditions play an influential role in the behaviour of the founder. However, the entrance of the younger generation introduces a variety of potential conflicts, having been educated and socialised in the West it would not be unreasonable to expect their attitudes towards the business and support services to be different, to the point of being inconsistent compared with those views expressed by their parents. One could argue that every generation has its own set of tensions and different ways of approaching issues, for example, approaches to conducting business, regardless of culture and geography. However, the underlying argument in this research considers the fact that the younger generation of South Asians born and/or raised in the West are exposed to two opposing cultural sets – the independence of the West as well as the family-first ethos of the East. These tensions are stressed during the emotional and turbulent period of transition and as each generation pulls the business in a separate direction, the final results can be catastrophic for the business and the family.

Over time the field of family businesses has increasingly moved towards a more integrated approach between the family and the business. It is this integration that is the starting point of work on Asian family firms where families and kinship networks are very close-knit and critical to all aspects of business development. The bonds of family and co-ethnic community are usually strengthened by migration and thereby create a stronger source of support for business development. Co-ethnic support is a double-edged sword, in addition to its advantages it can also be a limiting factor in the scope of the business and economic development of individuals. Economic success provides a springboard that enables migrant communities to achieve greater social integration and mobility often unachievable during migration of the first generation.

The contexts of Asian family businesses are a critical factor across all stages of their development. The cohesiveness of families (both immediate and extended) as well as kinsfolk from co-ethnic community are particularly vulnerable to the tensions and conflicts that arise during inter-generational succession. The negative effects can prompt the risk of destabilisation economically and socially not only within the family and the religious-ethnic community but also perhaps the wider business environment. In other countries the Asian business community has already faced succession, for example in Kenya the migrant Asian community is now facing succession from second to third generation. Deep-seated splits of the business between brothers and/or cousins commonly occur. Within the economy this then results in an increase in the number of firms competing within the same, often limited, market sharing both suppliers and competitors. The human experiences of these schisms within the business lead to rifts within the business that often persist beyond a single generation and have a deep effect on the stability and cohesion within the tight-knit religious-ethnic community.

The three Asian communities examined in this book have different experiences of migration and the countries they settle in. For the community in East Africa this was the first example of large-scale migration. The environment they faced was turbulent and economically uncertain but also provided significant opportunities for enterprise in a relatively under-developed economy. The large number of Asians who came to Britain in 1970s were mainly from East Africa – the mass migration initiated by forced expulsion from Uganda of fears of similar fates for this in neighbouring states. Britain was a far more developed economy, however employment opportunities were limited and once again entrepreneurship provided a means by which individuals could negotiate blocked opportunities. South Asian migration to the United States has increased over the last ten to twenty years. The individuals often came directly from the Indian sub-continent with the intention of exploiting the mature capitalist market and associated entrepreneurial opportunities.

In order to examine the working dynamic and future of Asian family firms it is important to generate a greater understanding of their context and also motivations for business start-up. The relationship between the founder and the business is a critical factor in inter-generational succession and as examples illustrate motivations for business start-up vary widely across the countries. The book is split into four sections, one for each country and the final section incorporating the conclusion and long-term development of the family firms. Each section that deals with a country has two chapters, the first presents the theoretical discourse and developments of entrepreneurship and family business activity amongst the South Asian community. The second section discusses specific issues on the working dynamics and survival of family firms in these communities. These discussions are generated from primary data collected from family firms in all three countries. Quotes from all the interviews have been used in the main body of the work and in addition three businesses from each country are presented as cases in the appendices. This provides additional reference or teaching material. The first section begins with the Kenyan Asian community, moving on to Britain followed by American South Asians.

The term 'Asian' in this book refers to people who originate from the Indian sub-continent, however for ease and consistency they have been referred to as South Asians wherever possible.

2
The South Asian Diaspora

Introduction

Asian settlement across the globe has been extensive, both in terms of geography and depth. Trading was the earlier impetus for movement as merchants sought out opportunities to conquer virgin territories. Over time this heritage has become a powerful force in the momentum of Asian migration particularly in the latter half of the twentieth century (Seidenberg, 1996). In the quest for new opportunities the Asian Diaspora has spread itself far and wide, thereby creating a broad network strengthened by economic and cultural ties. Through the institutionalisation of business activity, members of this migrant community have created an identity of entrepreneurial resilience, although this has been somewhat over-exaggerated in certain circumstances leading to claims of the Asian 'Midas touch'.

Experiences of re-settlement have been varied and often complex involving double and even triple migration. The main thrust of migration and subsequent shifts from the Indian sub-continent all have significant triggers propelling mass movement. In the first instance the split of India and creation of Pakistan led to communities and even families experiencing schisms as they were re-routed along boundaries of nationality and geography. These distinctions have become entrenched over time and affected migration and settlement patterns and even levels of socio-economic integration. Affiliation with community and religious groups all feed into the social capital and other resources available for economic development of these groups. Over time this is manifested in clear distinctions between groups in terms of how they have exploited these resources to their advantage. Figures highlight the highly successful nature of groups from East Africa, many of whom have experienced double-migration through their expulsion in the 1971 from Uganda and subsequent mass migration from Kenya and Tanzania (Mattausch, 1998; Tinker, 1977). As a comparison other groups from the Indian sub-continent, namely the Pakistani and Bangladeshi community, face problems of low educational attainment and low economic opportunities leading to limited socio-economic integration with the mainstream in the United Kingdom and elsewhere (Basu, 1995; Metcalf *et al.*, 1996). These two groups exemplify the polarisation of ethnic migrant success and integration. For the East African Asian community the experience of expulsion reinforced the need for migrants to adopt their new homeland more effectively and overtly and realise there was little chance of repatriation. Furthermore in many cases there was no desire to return to the Indian sub-continent as this was a place associated with their fore fathers holding little relevance or emotional attachment for the next generation.

Migrants from India and other parts of the sub-continent had less traumatic precursors to migration. On the whole this category of migrants were primarily motivated to improve their prospects by seeking employment and wealth abroad. Migration for these individuals followed a set pattern; younger men (married or single) would settle overseas, seeking employment often in low-skilled jobs. Their vision was to stay in their new country on a temporary basis whilst building up fortune before returning back to home. Castles and Kosack (1985) refer to such individuals as 'Sojourners':

> a sojourner is a person whose mental orientation is towards the home country. [He] spends a major portion of his lifetime striving for economic betterment and higher status, but the full enjoyment and final achievement of his objective is to be in his place of origin. (Lee, 1960, quoted in Watson, 1984: 5)

These individuals often found their return to home continuously delayed, until they became part of the migrant South Asian community in the United Kingdom, Canada or any other country other than their original home. As they became settled they would seek to establish a family base, either by bringing family members over or by finding partners from their co-ethnic communities in their new homes. Many of these individuals found themselves in a paradoxical situation; it was not the lure of their country that kept them from home, instead the realisation they could not afford to leave and return home in the style they had anticipated.

Settlement of the Asian community in different countries has led to varying degrees of integration and along with this greater fragmentation of the group into pre-existing subgroups classified according to religion and even geographical backgrounds. For a long time, research on Asian migrants in countries such as the United Kingdom and United States of America treated the community as a homogenous mass, applying broad-brush approach to their needs, both social and economic (Banks, 1996). However, since the mid-1990s, researchers have increasingly acknowledged the diversity of the Asian community and implications of this in terms of entrepreneurship and economic activity as well as educational differences (Modood and Berthoud, 1997). The divisions between members of the South Asian community were clearly defined in the 2001 Census and this has created a strong basis for quantitative data in this area.

From the sub-continent to East Africa

Trading under British Colonial rule was restricted and even discouraged in India as efforts were directed to encourage economic activity in Britain (Seidenberg, 1996). This often led to an increased number of merchants travelling to other countries for trading opportunities without the regulations and limitations imposed in the Indian sub-continent. Many traders followed the route from Bombay to the Kenyan island of Mombassa earning the title 'Mercantile Adventurers' (Seidenberg, 1996) travelling on dhows. This trade route was a long-established porthole into East Africa and beyond and held opportunities for entrepreneurs to prosper from under-developed economic territory (Patel, 1997). The position of Indians provided a critical factor as the different ethnic communities repositioned themselves in the late 1800s. As British rule decreased the vibrant Arab–Indian trade on the East African Coast, predominantly in Mombassa this created a vacuum in the economy, quickly filled by the entrepreneurial Asian community:

> The old period of Arab ascendancy was at end, the Indians were by far the dominant economic community at Zanzibar and along the East African coast. They constituted the vital middle class, which served as the connecting link on the eastern side of the continent between the African peoples and the peoples of Europe, America and Asia. They introduced the manufactured goods and technology of the industrial centres of the outside world to the indigenous Africans and they brought many of the natural recourse and agricultural products of the African interior to the international markets. (Patel, 1997: 9)

The arrival of Indians and Pakistanis to East Africa was a combination of opportunity-seekers who exploited the trading network between India and East Africa along with labourers. For the former group the migration to Kenya provided a means by which communities from lower castes in the Indian social system could return home and achieve upward mobility on the basis of their economic success abroad (Chandra, 1997). Many members of this group, particularly Patidars (Gujaratis) adopted the characteristics of 'Sojourners' (Castles and Kosack, 1985) emphasised by their practice of reinvesting wealth in land and buildings back home (Chandra, 1997). Tinker (1977) identified three main Indian groups that achieved improved social and economic mobility through migration to Kenya. His examples illustrate transition representing socio-economic advancement of groups within the migrant Asian community from a mainly proletarian to bourgeoisie level. The Sikh community responded most favourably through recruitment to a considerable number of posts within the police force. The second group, members of the Patidar community (mentioned above), moved from farming to rural trade and manufacturing, and finally the Patel caste replaced their businesses with professional jobs mainly in the public sector. However, the remainder of the Asian community had to find a means of sustaining themselves and their families, and this was achieved through entrepreneurship.

A large number of Indians were taken to East Africa for the explicit purpose of developing the region's infrastructure through building railroad tracks. Construction of the Ugandan Railway commenced in 1896 as the first cohort of Indian workers arrived in January of that year, ranging from skilled craftsmen to labourers (Hill, 1949). As numbers of Asians increased over the years so too did the opportunities for entrepreneurship.

For many Asians Mombassa provided the initial landing base through which they entered the country. Within five years the population in this area had swelled to 24,719. In 1890 the number of Asians in the area totalled 500, by 1895 this had increased to 863 residents, along with 4799 Punjabi labourers and 300 soldiers (Patel, 1997). Figures for migration into Kenya are somewhat limited in their accessibility, however Chandra (1997) has critiqued the migration patterns of Asians in and out of Kenya using data from 1911 to 1939. Peak levels of migration into Kenya occurred during 1924–1926. By 1931 the Indian population in Kenya had increased by 272 per cent and the Indian population as a whole stood at just over 50,000. The level of activity amongst entrants via Mombassa had also risen to over 3593 Indians in 1924 (Chandra, 1997).

By 1939 levels of outward migration had overtaken inward migration. This was a combined result of unfavourable economic conditions along with fear of hostility amongst the Indians (Chandra, 1997). Indian population levels still remained buoyant and continued to do so until 1960s and 1970s. Restrictions were placed to limit excessive numbers of Asians into Kenya in 1948 through The Immigration (Control) Ordinance; this was by no means the first time such limits had been imposed on the community. The uncertainty of the political and economical situation in Kenya combined with the temporary mindset adopted by migrants meant a large number of the Asian community were constantly looking for new opportunities. In 1962 the British Immigration Act restricted the entry of citizens from the Commonwealth, however those with British passports were exempt from these restrictions (Hiro, 1991). A year later Kenya achieved Independence (Uhuru). Colonial links provided a means by which East African Asians could continue to move forwards rather than returning home. A large number of Asians chose to move to the United Kingdom and those that did not maintain insurance retained their British passports and citizenship to the anger of the Kenyan government. From this period, during the 1960s, a series of events further deteriorated the stability of Asians in Kenya (e.g. the 1967 Immigration and Trade Licensing Act) as well as increasing restrictions on the movement of Asians into the United Kingdom (1968 The British Nationality Act). Similar practices were occurring across East Africa, including the Ugandan Immigration Act (1969), a precursor to the expulsions of Asians from Uganda in 1972.

The most recent figures on Asians in Kenya seem to be drawn from the 1989 Census (Bhushan, 1998). By this period the number of Asians in Kenya stood at 87,323 (including all categories of Asians). The breakdown of these figures is presented in Table 2.1. The overall total for the Asian population still suggests a sizeable population, however their proportion as part of the wider population emphasises the paradox between their lack of visibility and economic clout in the country.

Table 2.1   South Asian population in Kenya

	Population	% of total
Kenyan Asians	52,968	0.25
Indians	29,091	0.14
Other Asians	5264	0.02

Source: Bhushan (1998).

Migration to the United Kingdom

There has been a South Asian presence in the United Kingdom since the eighteenth century. Over time there have been four main phases that constitute periods of mass influx of Asians into the United Kingdom leading to the establishment of the British Asian community. Ballard and Ballard (1984) classified these periods into three main trends: the pioneer phase, the second wave, and the third phase and settlement. Prior to the Pioneering phase the South Asian community in the United Kingdom was negligible and very segregated. Indians, primarily Sikhs, who had joined the police and British Army were often posted overseas as part of their duty (Hiro, 1991). This helped to create and reinforce the momentum of movement and migration to other countries. The pioneer phase primarily consisted of ex-seamen and peddlers who became established in the United Kingdom during the two world wars (Anwar, 1977). After the First World War Britain was the only country in Europe that had maintained an 'open door' policy to immigrants. This led to a constant yet insignificant 'trickle' of Sikh immigrants (Hiro, 1991). Only those individuals fluent in English were able to secure jobs in factories, the rest, mainly craftsmen, became self-employed as peddlers selling an assortment of products door to door. The other sector of the Asian population comprised of students from India who were studying to be doctors before returning home. The outbreak of the Second World War led to the recruitment of many Indian doctors and graduate students who then stayed on as residents. Hiro (1991) estimates the Asian population in 1949 did not exceed 8000 of which 1000 were doctors.

The second wave after the Second World War occurred as a series of unrelated events unfolded; the partition of India and Pakistan in 1947 created displacement in both areas. Family members who became surplus to requirements in farming, particularly within the Sikh community, chose to move to Britain instead where they were immediately recruited into factory jobs requiring unskilled labour. The entrance of Asians in the 1950s was a relief for Britain, its economy was facing a substantial shortage of unskilled labour and these gaps were filled through recruitment of individuals from the Commonwealth colonies. Many of the migrants were recruited into jobs the indigenous populations were not willing to do (Layton-Henry, 1992). The influx of migrants during this period was so great that the immigrant population in the United Kingdom doubled during that period. Whilst certain groups such as the West Indian Community had already peaked with their migration levels, others such as the Asian community were only starting to generate a momentum for migration (Peach, 1996).

The third phase of migration for the Asian community is split over two decades, the first marked by the 1962 Commonwealth Immigrants Act. Prior to this legislation Commonwealth citizens had a great deal of flexibility to move between Britain and their homeland. This legislation forced individuals to commit to staying in one country; for many this meant choosing Britain as their home and forsaking the place of their ancestors in a bid for greater economic opportunities. Many 'sojourners' were forced to make a commitment and stay in Britain. Individuals who were already in the United Kingdom encouraged fellow kin-members to come over before the opportunities closed. This led to an unexpected scenario of imbalance between males and females; the 1961 Census showed the male–female ratios of Pakistanis and Indians in Bradford were 40:1 and 3:1 respectively (Hiro, 1991). The hysteria before the enactment of the 1962 Bill swelled the numbers of immigrants creating greater demands on the resources of the ethnic community already settled in Britain. The profile of migrants also shifted from educated individuals towards those from an agricultural background with little prior exposure to British culture or language. In spite of this Hiro (1991) argues the co-ethnic community still provided a strong sense of solidarity and support for continued chain migration;

> one factor remained constant throughout: the importance of the contact or sponsor in Britain. During the 'beat the ban' rush of 1961–2, the houses of early settlers virtually became receptions centres. (Hiro, 1991: 115)

The second part of the third phase occurred a decade later during the 1970s initiated by the arrival of economic refuges expelled from Uganda. Events leading up to the expulsion led to a mass exodus of Asians from neighbouring Kenya and Tanzania, who were terrified that they would suffer the same fate of having ninety-days notice to leave the country. Figures for the population of Ugandan Asians who settled in the United Kingdom vary from 30,000 (Bristow *et al.*, 1975) to 50,000 (Hiro, 1991). However, as Figure 2.1 illustrates, the influx of Ugandan Asians along with those from neighbouring East African created a significant rise in the number of Asians amongst the migrant ethnic population in Britain. Of these figures Hiro (1991) states estimates place at least 200,000 of Asians in Britain were from East and Central Africa. For many East African Asians Britain provided another place where they

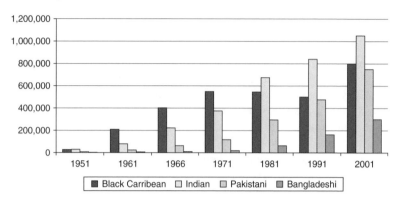

Figure 2.1 Population of selected ethnic groups in the United Kingdom (1951–2001).
Source: From the 1991 Census (Peach, 1996) and the 2001 Census (Strategy Unit, 2003).

could exploit opportunities and start flexing their trading skills. Although they came with varying amounts of financial capital, what they lacked in this area they over-compensated for in experience, acumen and social capital – namely human and intellectual.

The fourth phase of Asian settlement in the United Kingdom is described as emergence into adulthood of migrants and the growth of subsequent British-born generations (Ballard and Ballard, 1984). The majority of the Asian population is currently moving from second-generation British-born to third generation. Over time as subsequent generations have created their niche identities, politicians and researchers still focus on issues of identity, multi-culturalism (or even pluralism), but the debates have progressed beyond the simplistic views of integration versus assimilation towards the more subtle layers of the fabric of identity and the impact of religion as a definition of personality.

Motivations for entry and settlement to the United Kingdom were broad, ranging from forced expulsion to opportunistic seekers and 'sojourners' (Castles and Kosack, 1985). The experiences of 'sojourners' in Britain were similar to their counterparts in Kenya. They straddled both countries with a foot in each region often generating an income in Britain that was accumulated back home for the benefit of their family. This practice created the same resentment as it had in East Africa and was largely halted by the 1962 Commonwealth Immigrants Act. Although Asian migrants were still able to send money home, they were forced to commit to establishing a base in the United Kingdom and this required them to start investing more of their money in their new homeland. As members of the Asian community became established in Britain they created a new life for themselves. They had to adapt aspects of their traditional values and culture to co-exist with Western practices. Over time the 'sojourners' became permanent fixtures in the British Asian community not because they had inadequate funds for returning home but due to a gradual realisation that their arrival home would not generate the employment opportunities or even lifestyle they had craved.

On entering the United Kingdom the South Asian community faced hostile reactions for employment and living conditions (Watson, 1984; Ramdin, 1987; Iganski and Payne, 1996; Alibhai-Brown, 2000). Whilst members of the host community were reluctant to work in low-skilled jobs they resented the idea of foreigners coming in and taking their jobs. However, the reality was that when Britain faced such severe labour shortages the Government proactively encouraged the movement of cheap workers from the Indian sub-continent. Layton-Henry (1992) cites examples of adverts in the Indian press for workers in Woolf's rubber factory in Southall, West London, an area that still has a high settlement of Asians predominantly from the Punjab. For most of the indigenous population their only exposure of the Asian community had been within the parameters of the Colonial relationships, with Britain at the helm. It was therefore considered perfectly normal to create and maintain a class distinction between themselves and the migrants thereby replicating patterns of engagement during the colonial period (Castles and Kosack, 1985).

The response from the Asian community was complexity and astonishment. In many cases the background and experiences of the Asian migrants was vast, including those who had come from highly successful and prominent family business backgrounds in either East Africa or the sub-continent. In the face of this hostility the migrants had to find ways by which they could carve out their living, this often meant starting again from scratch. Settlement was dictated by employment availability, and as discussed previously the main sources of employment for Asian and other former Colonial migrants were factories.

Researchers present different accounts of the experiences of recruits into such organisations, particularly in the context of the background of Asian migrants and the lack of economic opportunities available to them on arrival. The profile most commonly associated with Asian migrants is one of strong qualifications and abundant experience (Ramdin, 1987). However, other researchers argue that claims of a highly skilled Asian migrant community are 'exaggerated' particularly amongst the community from East Africa (Mattausch, 1998). He goes on to argue that whilst a number of professionals were University graduates, the majority of the migrant community was composed of businessmen who had achieved 'low' levels of schooling. In many cases employment was low skilled with limited opportunities for promotion. The blocked upward mobility thesis is argued to be one of the critical factors influencing the significant levels of entrepreneurship amongst Asian migrants.

Discrimination was not limited to employment, and migrants found it equally difficult when seeking housing. In the 1950s and 1960s newly arrived migrants often found signs in accommodation stating 'No Coloureds, No Dogs' (Alibhai-Brown, 2000). Lack of secure employment created difficulties for individuals in these groups to get mortgages. Accommodation in many cases initially meant many men bunked up in single rooms in large numbers. However, as their families migrated they had to find suitable accommodation for their dependents. Through community resources a means of navigating this emerged as groups developed rotating credit circles. These projects worked on the basis of financial contributions from each member on a monthly basis until they had sufficient money for a house deposit. The circle would continue until all members had been able to raise sufficient money for each to have a deposit. The cohesiveness of tightly knit communities ensured members were obliged to repay their debts. The solidarity amongst ethnic communities reinforced through the experiences of migration and settlement created an important source of social capital that provided an important basis for business activity, as will be discussed in subsequent chapters.

Migration to and settlement in the United States of America

Asian migration to North and Central America was dominated by Asian migrants from 1978 onwards (Arnold *et al.*, 1987). Kanjanapan (1996) argues 40 per cent of immigrants from 1988 to 1990 have been Asians with those from India in the top five countries. Migration in the United States has been influenced by three main events that originate from the 1965 Immigration and Nationality Act. The legislation replaced the national origins quota system with a new visa preference system. The aim of this initiative was to encourage family reunification, followed by allowances for occupational skills and refugee status. The next amendment enabled migrants to emphasise family links as a basis for entry rather than required skills. The final modification was the introduction of the labour certification that was designed to ensure that immigrants had the skills required by the country. Asian migration to the United States has been dominated by skilled individuals, thereby representing a dominant group in the immigration of all professional individuals (Kanjanapan, 1996). Within this group skilled individuals from India were usually the dominant or second largest group across a range of professions including: Engineering, Maths and Computer Science, Natural Science and those in the Medical field.

The large-scale migration of professional has a knock-on effect on the range of individuals who also enter the country and their subsequent business activity. Individuals who entered through relatives did not have the qualifications or to enable recruitment into skilled jobs. However, the impact of family sponsorship created a large pool of human capital, an ideal base for business development:

> The post-World War II immigration waves to the United States and Canada have given rise to a reinvigorated small business sector in both societies. (Marger and Hoffman, 1992: 968)

The figures from the 2000 Census (Reeves and Bennett, 2004) generate an up-to-date profile of the American South Asian community. Figures estimate the Asian population to have reached just over ten million, a 68 per cent rise since 1990. Seventeen per cent of this figure is made up of Indians and Pakistanis (Reeves and Bennett, 2004). This profile presents the ideal demographic for engaging in high-growth economic activity. The group has a higher proportion of men and women compared to the total population in the young adult age group (20–39 years) (Reeves and Bennett, 2004).

The South Asian population as a whole is still relatively new to the United States. Figures drawn from the 2000 Census show the majority of individuals entered the United States between 1990 and 2000. Just over half of the American South Asian population entered during this period, with 54 per cent from India and 58.5 per cent from Pakistan. This contrasts sharply with migration patterns of other Asian communities to the United States who settled before 1989; for example, 83 per cent of Cambodians, 64 per cent of Filipinos, 63 per cent of Thai, 62.6 per cent of Korean and 57.3 per cent of Chinese (Reeves and Bennett, 2004). These figures show migration both directly from the Indian sub-continent and through East Africa is not synchronised with patterns to the United Kingdom, other Western European countries and even Canada.

Settlement of the wider Asian American community is largely in ethnic enclaves (Auster and Aldrich, 1984) across the United States. These may not be as concentrated as settlements of Asians in the United Kingdom, however a number of states are characterised by established Asian communities. The two most common areas of South Asian settlement are California and New York, housing 64 per cent of the population (Reeves and Bennett, 2004). In addition large Asian communities can be found in Washington, Virginia, Texas, Florida, Hawaii, New Jersey, Massachusetts and Illinois (Reeves and Bennett, 2004).

Education once again becomes a key factor in the development of the South Asian community. South Asian Americans in general are praised for their ability to overcome discrimination by achieving high levels of success through education (Le, 2001). However, he continues to argue that a more detailed account of the situation highlights significant disparities between groups with Chinese and South Asians performing far better than Southeast Asians. Comparisons across ethnic migrant communities show higher numbers of Indian (63.9%) and Pakistanis (54.3%) achieving a Bachelor's degree than other ethnic groups, the next highest figure is the Chinese community (48.1%). The achievement of education inevitably has implications across all sections of the community, ranging from increased professional opportunities to a broader and more effective base from which businesses develop and operate family firms.

The Asian Diaspora had spread beyond these countries and continues to grow. The links of family and kinship remain across continents providing a critical source of human capital for business development. The experiences of migration described in these three countries reinforce the importance of chain migration as a means supporting new arrivals and creating a strong co-ethnic support. Support offered through the co-ethnic communities is critical for emotional and cultural empathy as well as the more pragmatic business development and domestics needs. The following chapters will provide examples of how co-ethnic resources and associated forms of capital have been critical in helping to generate some of Asian dynasties that are critical to a range of business environments.

3
Dreams of Dynasties – Business Start-up in Kenya

Introduction

The economy in Kenya and indeed the neighbouring East African states is a combination of trading routes from the Indian sub-continent and migrant entrepreneurial activity that flourished under extremely volatile political conditions of Colonialism and subsequent Independence. It would not be an exaggeration to state that the backbone of the Kenyan economy for a long time has been the entrepreneurial drive from the Asian population. This chapter describes the conditions in which Asian businesses first emerged and then prospered in Kenya. As with figures on Asian migration, the data in this area is sparse and fragmented. The reasons for this is primarily due to the relative inaccessibility of the East African Asian business community. Their insularity and lack of presence is notable in the national press, wide range of academic research and even government-based business support initiatives. This has led to Asians being dubbed as the 'missing middle' (Ferrand, 1996). The sections in this chapter focus on motivations and circumstances surrounding business start-up, with a particular focus on the social capital utilised during entrepreneurial activities and business start-up and development.

The Kenyan economy

There is little doubt that the Asian population has been a powerful driving force behind Kenya's economy (Himbara, 1994). Their success, however, has not been without considerable struggle. The previous chapter chartered the experiences and trends of migration from the Indian sub-continent to Kenya. Working on the East African railways led to wide dispersal of the migrant Asian community. The strength of Asian social capital, drawing on links both from back home and across Kenya and even East Africa generated business opportunities that visionary individuals were able to exploit. These business opportunities soon permeated beyond the Asian community to service the needs of the wider population and in turn resulted in their monopoly of the trading market. In many ways Asian entrepreneurs provided the bedrock of the new economy in Kenya. Their business activity penetrated all aspects of society and traversed all ethnic backgrounds:

> Thus apart from a few early British chain stores, almost right from the beginning most of the retail trade was in the hands of Asian merchants who supplied the smaller Asian traders with practically every commodity that was used in the three East African territories of Kenya, Uganda and Tanganyika. (Seidenberg, 1996: 35)

Until the early 1920s the Indian rupee was the common form of currency circulating through East Africa, the most potent representative of the Indian monopoly on trading activity (Mattausch, 1998). Commerce was in its infancy as the Kenyan market was developing and Asians were quick to spot untapped markets benefiting from first entrant advantage. Asian business development was largely unhindered as they had no serious direct competition. Africans did not have the trading experience, networks or access to financial resources and the ruling European class looked upon business activities with condescension:

> Although Britain was often identified as a 'nation of little shopkeepers', in East Africa simple trading generally was avoided by Europeans... not the type of a proper gentleman should do. (Seidenberg, 1996: 121)

> The entire country had grown up on the Indian trader... Without him the whole economy would have collapsed like a burst balloon. (Himbara, 1994: 40–41)

Hence Asian business activity was not perceived as a threat, instead this group was regarded as a powerless middle class who merely operated small enterprises at the lower end of the economy. Experiences in Colonial India had emphasised the consequences of being in a vulnerable position, and the Asian community began to capitalise on their strengths. For many East African Asians their potential survival and prosperity lay in trading:

> early Asian settlers were continuing a time-honoured tradition... bereft of political power and armed only with commercial acumen they were building businesses, whilst others were building empires. (Mattausch, 1998: 123)

Whilst the Europeans focused their attention on farms, Asian traders were able to establish a prosperous foothold in the East African economy. Himbara (1994) ascribes the following characteristics to the Asian community: significant commercial awareness, sheer determination and hard work along with strong forms of social capital. These factors provide a strong base underlying the community's tenacity to survive and prosper in remote areas and develop foundations for economic growth. The proliferation of such 'dukhawallahs'[1] established the roots of many current Asian giants that helped to shape not only the Kenyan, but also the East African economies.

During the colonial period in Kenya the Asians occupied an intermediary role between the native Africans and the ruling British. Tinker (1977) describes how the class system in colonial Kenya was divided amongst the ethnic groups; Europeans populated government and senior positions, Asians a small proportion in middle administrative and commerce jobs, whilst the Africans were employed as labourers and for menial jobs. This system of racial segregation ensured that the Africans were retained at the lowest levels with limited or no opportunities of socio-economic advancement. The divisions between the groups were firmly entrenched and managed to ensure limited 'leakage' especially upwards. Twenty per cent of Asians occupied elite professional and administrative posts (Tinker, 1977).

Inevitably the strong hierarchical structure between the ethnic groups created tensions and resentment. The Asian community found itself in a particularly precarious position as it buffered the hostility between the ruling British and the native Kenyans. The Asians did not behave in a manner that eased the tumultuous relations, instead the community opted for greater segregation and retreated even further into their own communities (Seidenberg, 1996). This behaviour is often ascribed to communities who are under threat and face common enemies through strengthening their bonds of cohesion (Coser, 1968). Religious and even class (or caste) distinctions were negotiated as Asians joined forces in the face of common adversity: 'groups constitute themselves only through conflict and become aware of their interests in and through conflict' (Coser, 1968: 34). However, in this instance Tinker (1977) argued the Asians were not completely passive victims in the roles they played within society: 'the Asians accepted little of the interpersonal freedom of the British whom they morally despised, and nothing from the Africans whose cultural existence they ignored' (Tinker, 1977: 96).

The increasing economic success of the Asian community along with their self-imposed isolation led to greater disharmony. This highly segregated approach to living irked the excluded African community in particular who resented the overt displays of wealth amongst the community. It would be unfair to apply this attitude to all East African Asians, however the events post-independence that created greater vulnerability for Asians were a combination of strong emotions, frustration and freedom from repression, which generated extreme reactions from the Africans. It was far easier for the Africans to blame the Asians for their position of poverty rather than the Europeans. Post-Kenyan Independence (Uhuru) saw relations between Asians and Africans severely deteriorated with dire consequences:

> Caught in between the immediate past and the struggle for responsible self-government, Indians had to accept an independent East Africa without any special protection for minorities. (Seidenberg, 1996: 176)

Despite many sectors of the Asian community joining forces with the Africans in their struggle to gain Independence, once this was achieved it was a bittersweet victory for the Asians. African grievances towards Asians intensified, they resented the relative comfort and wealth of the Asian community. Furthermore, they felt Asians were not committed to Kenya, primarily as many Asians refused to relinquish their British passports for Kenyan ones. Independence enabled Africans to rectify what they perceived to be injustices of colonialisation and their closest and easiest target was the Asian community. Senior Asian professionals were removed from prestigious jobs, whilst others found it increasingly difficult to retain or get jobs in any sectors of the civil service (Tinker, 1977). Once again the Asian community had to consider a change in career path and, for many, entrepreneurship or entering the family business became a very attractive, if not the only career choice.

'Africanisation' had been intended to produce an African capitalist class, however, as Himbara (1994) comments, it led to unexpected effects. The Asian community initially withdrew from commerce and trading, moving into construction and manufacturing. Although a limited number remained in retailing, this economic shift left significant gaps within the market. Many Africans that entered these markets did not have the skills, experience or contacts that enabled them to emulate the business success of the Asian community. Often the new African entrepreneurs were at best partly skilled and found it difficult to make the transition to business ownership. The failure of African businesses to conquer these markets led to regenerated opportunities for Asians to return to the heart of commerce, thus reinforcing the Asian grip on the economy:

> Micro-enterprises are indigenous while the medium-sized and larger manufacturing enterprises are dominated by Asian (Indian) capital. (Gray *et al.*, 1997: 68)

Although Asian business activity has helped to resuscitate the Kenyan economy, the Africans became even more resentful of what they felt to be a denial of their rights for economic advancement. Unsurprisingly this reaction generated increased hostility and greater uncertainty for the safety of the Asian community across East Africa. This reached crisis point in 1972 when the Ugandan President Idi Amin ordered the expulsion of Asians from Uganda within ninety days. This sent waves of panic amongst neighbouring East African states where African–Asian relations were already strained. Although, Kenya and Tanzania had not implemented such drastic measures, Asians feared for their safety and, if had not already done so, began moving vast amounts of money abroad.

In spite of these extreme measures the Asian community was not totally extinguished in Kenya or Tanzania. As discussed in the previous chapter, a number of families decided to remain, either because of business opportunities or because they were in situations where investments could not be easily liquidated. Despite the considerable reduction of the size of the population, the shrunken Asian community maintained its grip on the economy through entrepreneurship. Embedded ethnic networks and social capital have continued to provide critical resources to successive generations. Through this consolidation and active engagement of co-ethnic resources the Asian presence in the economy is argued to far outweigh their physical numbers in Kenya (Akumu, 1996; Omwoyo, 1996).

Although Government activity post-independence was targeted towards encouraging Africans to emulate Asian entrepreneurial success the overall effect has been disappointing. African businesses have conquered the micro-enterprise sector with the proliferation of shops known as *Jua Kali*.[2] The sectoral differences of African and Asian businesses were further reinforced by ethnic-specific support services. Formal Enterprise agencies such as KMAP[3] focused their support on African businesses, whilst Asians relied on embedded ethnic networks described as part of entrepreneurial social capital (Rath, 2000; Kloosterman *et al.*, 1999). The lack of formalised support for Asian businesses reinforced the precarious position of Asian businesses in Kenya and this is still largely true today.

Whilst they are central to the economy, Asian businesses are not formally recognised by the Government and therefore do not benefit from resources beyond their own ethnic networks. Over time the population has dwindled as large numbers of the younger generation are sent overseas to North America and the United Kingdom for their university education. In many cases they are not encouraged to return home, but instead create links for future chain migration to the West. This 'silent exodus' (*The Economist*, 11.9.99) is likely to have a profound effect on the Kenyan economy over the longer term as Asian family firms start to suffer a decline in potential successors. This situation provides an interesting irony as simultaneously extensive efforts are invested into repatriation programmes for Ugandan Asians in an attempt to attract wealth back into Uganda.

Entrepreneurship and business development

The lack of employment prospects meant that for many Asians entrepreneurship or involvement in co-ethnic business was the only viable option to generate an income. As a result many of these individuals were 'pushed' into entrepreneurship. However this is balanced with typical arguments presented as 'pull' factors, namely resources generated through the social capital of the ethnic community. Business start-up created an opportunity to utilise ethnic networks and business opportunities these generated. In addition embedded ethnic networks provided a cheap base for the development of businesses. These resources enabled Asian enterprises to operate at a competitive advantage and, more importantly, handle money and daily activities with high levels of trust.

Businesses were generated as family members (often male) pooled their human and financial capital. The advantage of what were often larger number of family members meant there were more hands to oversee the daily activities of the business and monitor the daily income. The involvement of family is cited as a critical resource for business development and this is particularly emphasised in South Asian and other migrant ethnic firms (Boissevain *et al.*, 1990; Ram and Holliday, 1993; Basu, 1999). The survival and growth of the business was paramount as it provided the basis of stability for the family and even the wider community.

The reliance on various forms of capital – human, intellectual, financial and business experience – enabled Asians to penetrate a vast range of sectors. Retailing, in particular food and clothing, was an obvious choice. Over time, however, business activity expanded into less populated areas of retailing and wholesaling such as construction and furnishings. Eventually Asian businesses expanded across a range of sectors, covering service, trading and even manufacturing industries. Each sector still had barriers to entry. Drawing on resources from co-ethnic resources provided a means by which a number of these hurdles could be managed. Businesses also developed diverse portfolios, whereby families had sufficient capital (both human and financial) to invest in businesses across diverse sectors; ranging for example from Dry Cleaning to Tourism. In addition family businesses also became more confident about geographical expansion, moving across East Africa into Tanzania and Uganda before the 1972 expulsion.

As the business flourished so too did the wealth of the Asian community who in turn provided the primary customer base for many co-ethnic businesses. The success of the Asian community was a stark contrast to the native African population and exacerbated pre-Independence ethnic segregation. Relations between Africans and Asians became even more strained leading to greater economic and employment uncertainty amongst the East African Asian community.

Many of the founders who established businesses had very low education levels and so business was the only viable option to enable them to generate stability and income for themselves and their families. One of the traits of ethnic entrepreneurship, the 'copycat' effect whereby members emulate the enterprising efforts of pioneers was perpetuated. This process was less risky for entrepreneurs as they could build upon the previous experiences of co-ethnic members and minimise some of the risks. The business became the primary focus of activity, hence maintaining and achieving growth for the business became paramount in the wider context of greater unemployment and economic uncertainty. It was not uncommon for the younger generation to leave formal education without qualifications in order to work in the business. The likelihood of attending university for many was a distant dream both in terms of finances and educational levels. This created a large pool of resources, particularly in terms of family members who were groomed to enter the family business from a young age and had not considered any other career options.

> I was very young when I joined the business. I didn't have much of a chance to think about what I wanted to do, I knew my father wanted my help in the business and I was the eldest son, so it was my duty to help . . . At that time it was expected that the younger generation would go into the business, so staff expected it as well.

I had always expected to join the business. This is a family tradition and all the male kids were expected to join. I had finished my studies and didn't want to go on to further studies. My heart was in the business ... The rest of the family expected me to join the business, I think there would have been stronger reactions if I had decided not to!

My father had started up the business and it was growing faster than he had expected, he needed me in the business and so I decided to leave school and join the business. My younger brother joined the business a couple of years after I did, he also decided to leave school, we both knew eventually we would be in the family business so there didn't seem to be much point in delaying it.

The above quotes illustrate how younger family members were expected to fulfil their filial obligations by joining the business, often at the expense of their education. The businesses at this stage required trustworthy manpower in order to consolidate business activity and achieve growth. The lack of external employment opportunities coupled with the needs of the business meant that business entry was the natural progression for many second-generation entrants. The business thrived from the influx of willing and committed family members, what they had lacked in knowledge they more than compensated for in enthusiasm. However, large numbers of family members working together in a business with no formal strategies to manage working relationships created problems for the business and the family. In these situations there was a great deal of ambiguity in terms of succession strategies or even a clear allocation of control and power (below the founder and/or the father), this inevitably created tensions, not only between the generations but also amongst separate factions within families. These are factors that have been found to have dire effects on the survival of family firms (Rosenblatt *et al.*, 1985).

Resources available for business development

The range of manpower available to family businesses was vast and has already been cited as a significant factor in the extraordinary growth and dominance of Asian businesses across East Africa. In Kenya the settlement patterns of the Asian community broadly reflected religious groups or geographical affiliation. Within each community informal structures developed that infiltrated social, economic and religious aspects of the Diaspora. The experiences of migration and settlement and ensuing hostility from the host community had generated a very strong bond of social cohesion across the Asian community. The infrastructure for public services in Kenya as with other East African countries was poor and gaps in provisions provided opportunities for Asians to institutionalise their community-based organisations. For example schools were launched to offer improved educational opportunities for children, additionally hospitals were established to offer a higher standard of medical service. Often these facilities were restricted solely to community members, thereby reinforcing the divide between the ethnic groups. However, certain other communities offered their facilities to the wider community and created positive links across ethnic groups as well as initiating momentum for other Asian communities to follow:

> hospitals, colleges and schools were built, often by the Ismailis, the community whose increasing liberalism and "Westernisation" set a role model of progress for other Asian groups. (Mattausch, 1998: 129)

The impact of these institutions had a number of additional benefits. They reinforced the identity of Asians and often distinguished each religious-ethnic community. The recognition of distinct communities was perhaps easier in countries such as Kenya due to the prevailing tribal system that has remained integral to the social standing and attitudes of native Kenyans (Spring, 2002). More importantly these institutions provided a basis of stability for the Asians in the political turbulent environment. By providing facilities to support the wider population the Asian community was able to reinforce its position as an integral part in the social, economic and welfare provisions of the country. Having learnt form the mistakes of their segregation in Uganda, the single most important means of ensuring their stability in Kenya was through economic and social integration.

The support provisions that were prioritised in terms of resource allocation were those targeting basic needs of heath and education. Business support initiatives were very sparse and operated in a less cohesive manner. As described previously limited government-based provisions offered to micro-enterprises favoured entrepreneurship amongst native Kenyans. This is still the prevailing attitude in Kenya. Therefore, business support for Asian entrepreneurs and family businesses was derived from embedded ethnic networks – namely social capital from community-based resources and kinship networks and still continues in this form. In certain cases the infrastructure of the community means the nature of business support is often highly evolved thereby matching the needs of the businesses. The links generated and reinforced through various stages of migration have enabled participants to take advantage of strong networks across the Diaspora, to identify and develop business opportunities. Within Kenya the limited sources of formalised business support inevitably means resources are scarce. This is compounded with a highly fragmented social and cultural environment and long-standing tensions leading to significant mistrust between different ethnic communities. Asian businesses responded by continuing to draw on their co-ethnic resources. A common example is illustrated through manpower for the business; the structures are typically arranged in a hierarchical format. The positions that require significant trust are only offered to family members or close kin ties. Co-ethnic members occupy the less senior but supervisory roles. The posts requiring more menial labour are usually offered to members of different ethnic communities, namely native Africans. These business practices reinforce the hierarchical nature of ethnic positioning in Kenya and they also do very little to reduce the tensions amongst groups. Within the economy Asian businesses still retain a substantial amount of control and power. Resentment towards this derives from the inability of other ethnic groups to penetrate the enclaves and compete with these businesses.

Over time Asian businesses have had to face a number of challenges due to a complex combination of changes both in their external and internal environments. As the third generation of family members enter the business they are equipped with higher levels of education and exposure to working practices in other organisations and even other countries. In addition the environment of the business has changed and the wider workforce has also improved its education levels. Furthermore, directors in family businesses have had to accept significant cultural shifts in attitudes towards the workforce – in terms of family, non-family, co-ethnic and other ethnic communities. Such changes have been critical to implement practices that enable the businesses to survive and progress. These dynamics have occurred in the Kenyan Asian family firms whilst families and the business have also had to negotiate their way around inter-generational succession, as discussed in the next chapter.

Notes

1. Dukhawallah is a term commonly used to describe shopkeepers of Asian descent, dukha meaning shop in Gujarati.
2. Jua Kali – Swahili term for Hot Sun, refers to makeshift shops selling local hand-made crafts.
3. KMAP – Kenya Management Assistance Programme.

4
Growth and Succession in Kenyan Asian Family Firms

Introduction

Family businesses are perhaps the most complex form of organisation resulting from the interaction of three systems: the business, the owner and the family. As these three bodies collide interactions can vary from innovative and creative processes to destructive and emotionally turbulent power games. This chapter discusses various aspects of family business survival and growth during the inter-generational period. The cases from Kenya had already survived the experience of transition from the first to the second generation. The issues that emerged from these cases presented a combination of problems, some of which were common to any business experiencing transition regardless of their stage on the business life cycle, whilst others were more applicable to mature businesses. The main areas identified and discussed in this section are: choosing successors and the entry of the younger generation – with a particular focus on daughters, managing business growth, resolving disputes and the role of non-family staff, their involvement and relationship with younger family members. The chapter begins with an evaluation of the theory and developments on the dynamics in family firms.

The dynamics of family firms

The constant interaction of families and businesses often creates highly emotive experiences for all involved. The field of family business research has navigated its way through areas such as succession, growth and survival (Kuratko, 1995; Reid *et al.*, 1999), however the common strand connecting these areas is the nature of familial dynamics in businesses (Handler and Kram, 1988; Dyer and Handler, 1994; Dyck *et al.*, 1999). Researchers such as

Sharma *et al.* (1996), Poutziouris and Chittenden (1996), and Fournier and Lightfoot (1996) have highlighted the conflicting nature of families and businesses. This debate has illustrated the critical tension between the two bodies questioning where the emphasis lies – a family in business or a business in the family (Poutziouris and Chittenden, 1996). Ward (1987) highlights the inherent differences of the two systems leading to a contradictory existence – businesses are objective forms whilst families are emotional and less rational. This distinction leads to a number of opposing practices; families will be more protective over their members than businesses and are more likely to grant acceptance unconditionally whilst businesses will assess an individual's contribution before approving their membership.

This situation creates a number of issues and associated tensions whereby family and business issues compete for priority. Inevitably individuals who are in senior positions will make decisions and these are likely to be family members, their challenge lies in managing the somewhat conflicting nature of family and business needs. As a means of clarifying this relationship Taiguri and Davis (1982) developed the three-ringed model (Figure 4.1). The model represents the overlap between the three systems: the family, the business and the owner. The intersections represent the fluidity of the individual's ability to move between these systems. Each area of interaction represents a complex and highly emotive relationship between individuals or groups. The overlap of work and personal lives often means that achieving separation between these areas can be very difficult if not possible and when it does occur it is quite traumatic.

The previous chapter emphasised the significance of ethnic embedded networks (Kloosterman *et al.*, 1999) and the various forms of capital generated that are central to business development. Hence, when analysing

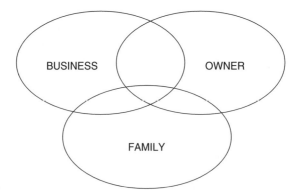

Figure 4.1 The three-ringed model.
Source: Taiguri and Davis (1982).

a family business it is important to acknowledge the impact of wider kin, the extended family and co-ethnic network. Support enabling business growth and development is not limited to a single action or event, instead resources provide ongoing help leading to greater embeddedness within the co-ethnic network (Janjuha-Jivraj, 2003). This behaviour is derived from the way in which individuals view themselves vis-à-vis their family. Bjerke (1998) argues the basic unit of currency in the West is the individual where as in Asian cultures it is the family. This attitude underpins behaviours and development of all aspects of individuals. Furthermore, societal differences between the West and the East greatly contribute to these cultural differences. This is explained by Wilson (1985) who emphasises the gap between first-generation migrants and their children due to significantly differing childhood and experiences of adolescence:

> It must also be remembered that many of the first-generation immigrants grew up in societies where there was no such thing as adolescence or youth culture. (Wilson, 1985: 79)

This leads to two important distinctions when considering key influences on family firms of Asian origin: first, there is little or no separation between the owner and the family; and secondly, wider kinship circles cannot be ignored. It is therefore necessary to adapt the three-ringed model to take account of these factors as illustrated in the community-contextualised model (Figure 4.2). The basic assumption underpinning

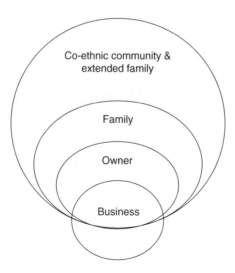

Figure 4.2 Community-contextualised model.

this model argues that the owner is firmly embedded in the family with no scope for long-term division or distinction. The links with co-ethnic community and extended family may fade over time with successive generational settlement and integration, however this is not always an automatic development.

Entry of the younger generation – From founder to successor

A significant number of family businesses in Kenya were generated from the need to create a stable base for the business as well as ensuring that younger family members had attractive viable career opportunities. It may not have been the specific intention of the entrepreneurs to create multi-generational dynasties, however external forces along with ethnic embedded networks created opportunities for businesses to flourish over many generations. As discussed in the previous chapter many public sector professional opportunities were closed to Asians. Furthermore, Kenyan commerce was still very under-developed with limited opportunities in international corporations located in the country. The limited scope of economic options combined with strong filial obligation meant that many families automatically assumed their children (namely, their sons) would enter the business. The entry considered a lifetime commitment as they had the long-term aim of eventually taking over the business. As previously discussed this affected the education of many second-generation Asians who left school before their education was complete. In spite of explicit expectations by family members and constant grooming from a young age a number of these individuals struggled with their own personal desires and the need to fulfil filial obligations:

> when my brother decided not to join the business it was unheard of then. My family was shocked. It was like they went into mourning. My father worked very hard to support the family, joining the business was seen as the son's duty.

> I had always expected to join the business. This is a family tradition and all the kids were expected to join. I had finished my studies and didn't want to go on to further studies. My heart was in the business.

During this period founders often had a great deal of choice when choosing successors. Whilst this created many opportunity the situation also generated its specific problems for the businesses and families who operated in a very tight-knit environment. These bonds of social cohesion led to considerable opportunities to utilise capital for business development. The literature on social capital, and in particular the work on ethnic networks, has focused a great deal on the impact of reciprocity and obligation amongst community members. As support is offered, the emphasis on members is not always on direct obligation, instead it is the context of donors and recipients that creates an important understanding of how the support will be reciprocated as (Durkheim, 1984). Within the Asian community help is accepted on the basis that the obligation generated from this action does not necessarily take the form of direct payback to provider. Instead benefits can be accrued through indirect actions, such as improved status amongst the community. Portes (1998) argues social pressure amongst such collectives is so strong that it creates an obligation on members to behave within acceptable norms. This creates greater sources of social capital generated from amongst the community and minimises deviant behaviour:

> social capital is not contingent on direct knowledge of their benefactor, but on membership in the same group . . . In other words trust exists in this situation precisely because obligations are enforceable, not through recourse to law or violence but through the power of the community. (Portes, 1998: 28)

As social capital created opportunities for the development of businesses the support offered also adapted to the needs of growing businesses and more importantly the notion of social co-ethnic support became embedded in migrant ethnic communities. This form of reciprocity led to chains of support providing assistance for subsequent families who required help within the community. One of the more common ways in which this manifested itself was through absorbing familial and kinship members into the business. The businesses at this stage generally required trustworthy manpower relying on individuals who were able to competently manage different tasks rather than specialise in one particular area. The management structure of these businesses was often very patriarchal and well suited to the involvement of family members. Co-ethnic labour was also treated as extended familial labour due to emotional and cultural proximity of the individuals in relation to the founder and founder's family.

The resources required for business start-up were a combination of financial and human capital, drawn in the first instance from the immediate and extended kinship circle. It was not uncommon for two or more brothers to pool their skills and resources in order start up a business. Whilst the founding brothers were in control the business benefited from their stability, shared vision and commitment to long-term development. The more developed businesses were able to take advantage of this management structure by dividing up areas each headed by a family member working independently but in synchronisation with the other divisions. The entry of the younger generation, however, inevitably created rivalries through insecurities. Cases where older nephews joined the business earlier created tension as the uncles were worried that their interests for their children (i.e. younger cousins) would be compromised as the older cousins would be well settled in the business. This tension often manifested itself in aggressive behaviour towards his siblings involved in the business and the younger generation. The quotes below illustrate how the sibling rivalry that had been initiated during the entry of the first generation affected the entry of the second generation:

> My Uncles had been in the business since the beginning. I was the new boy and the first of my generation to join. My father was more sympathetic to my problems and had more understanding with me...My Uncles were resentful of this I think. I tried to grin and bear it because I was expected to respect my elders.

> I was the eldest to join the business and it was expected that I would join, but I think my brothers resented it and were fearful that I would take the whole business away. Of course this didn't happen, but they didn't make things easy between my father and me. Eventually they joined the business, but when my son came in there were more problems, it is a bit easier now, but there are still problems.

> [When I joined the business] there was a lot of aggression. My father brought me into the business, but others, my uncles wouldn't take my ideas. I was given no authority for a long time. My father was very protective over me because of my uncles' behaviour.

In addition to the considerable body of research focusing on aggressive father–son dynamics, the other main thrust of work on familial dynamics has emphasised the destructive nature of sibling rivalry during generational transition (Kets de Vries, 1996). The tensions created through sibling rivalry are potentially detrimental to the survival of the business and this was particularly evident across many of the Kenyan cases.

The experiences of first generational transition resulted in long-standing grievances that were not always completely resolved as illustrated above. This was often exacerbated by the lethal combination of high emotional tension and lack of alternative career prospects, reinforced by the younger generation's premature departure from education. Many of these business were struggling to establish themselves and achieve stability, facing problems typical of a business moving along its life cycle coupled with operating in a highly turbulent political environment. Often family members did not possess the skills required to manage familial relationships within the context of a business. The focus had been completely directed towards generating experience relating specifically to the operations of the business and customer management. Amongst the second-generation entrants there was only one case where the successor had attended a management course at an American business school. It is no surprise this case provided the most open and advanced relationship between the first- and the second-generation successors and their management of the work–home interface.

Negotiating inter-generational transition from first to second generation did not mean the businesses were clear of family conflicts. The rivalries between siblings intensified with the entrance of the next generation and the businesses were not always able to withstand the familial conflict. A common 'solution' was to divide the business amongst the founding brothers. This happened in a number of the cases resulting in family rifts becoming entrenched through business schisms. The impact of these rifts were not limited to the business and immediate family, instead they created a ripple momentum whereby extended family and co-ethnic and even wider ethnic communities were affected. There was also a significant impact on the economy, these large businesses were cleaved but remained in the same industry, often using the same suppliers and fighting over the same customers. Inevitably this diluted their power in the market place and created greater uncertainty and instability for employment and growth potential.

Passing on the mantle – From second to third generation

The entry of the third generation into the family businesses reflected a marked distinction in the dynamics between family members and businesses. Unlike the second generation, business entry was not always considered the first or most attractive career option for the third generation. The greater stabilisation achieved in business following first- to second-generational transition had led to significant growth and market share.

This in turn created greater opportunities for family members, in particular improving educational prospects for the younger generation. Many of the second generation were keen not to enforce entry obligations they had experienced, often at the expense of their education, with their children. This meant the younger generation had opportunities to study abroad and continue their education without the pressure of being expected to join the business and sacrificing educational opportunities.

This shift in attitude towards familial entry between the generations illustrates an important departure from the traditional relationship between family members and the business especially over the longer term. The younger generation were encouraged to consider alternative career options. In spite of this there were instances where the previous generations exerted considerable pressure on the third generation. In some of these cases the younger respondents expressed frustration at the demands of the family and this in turn had a detrimental effect on familial working dynamics. The following pair of quotes shows how both generations viewed the entry of the third generation in one such case:

> I was groomed to join the business, it had always been expected of me from a young age that I would join the business. It is different for the new generation, they have full options whether or not join. My son had full choice. Family businesses are a way of life with their own tensions. You need to enter with an open heart to do well ... I didn't have a choice in entering the business, I want my children to have a choice ... No one should be obliged to make commitments to the business.

> From a very young age my grandfather would talk about me running the company. Through my education my father played an active role in encouraging me to take up studies that help the business, for example my choice of Degree [Commerce] ... Because of the emphasis on continuing in the business I knew I would have feelings of guilt if I didn't join the family business.

Despite such strong sentiments from the father towards his son's entry the younger generation still felt forced into the business, by both his father and grandfather. This tension was never completely resolved (Case K1, Appendix 1). The son found it very difficult to achieve harmonious and productive working relationships both with his father and even senior management. Where the younger generation had not been groomed nor developed expectations to join the business their entry to join the business followed their experiences of having worked elsewhere. Entry into the business was based on mutual consent. Furthermore, the experiences of the younger generation, having worked elsewhere before joining the business, enabled them to enter the business with greater confidence and credibility. The triggers for younger generation entry into the business are critical influences on subsequent working relationships. The feelings illustrated above illustrate a strong dichotomy between both generations in attitudes towards the entry of the younger generation. His father (a second-generation entrant) described how although his entrance into the business was expected he still felt his privileged position set him apart:

I know they felt I had been born with a silver spoon in my mouth.

The timing of younger generation entry into family business was critical. As discussed earlier the second generation joined the businesses during a period of tremendous upheaval. Most of the businesses had a very old and loyal workforce; in some cases, non-family staff had been with the businesses during their initial start-up stages. In certain cases entrance of the second generation was welcomed by family and staff. It had been expected, and non-family employees were relieved by this continuity and familial commitment during turbulent periods in the business life cycle:

They [non family employees] didn't seem to have much of a reaction. They worked for my father or grandfather and they would work for me. That's how things were done.

It was expected somehow that I would join the business and it was a mutual fit...They [non family employees] were very positive, they felt the new generation was coming in to the business. There was a little apprehension because new blood was coming in and they were worried about their jobs. But they know our family and our ethics well. My joining blended in beautifully because I didn't impose radical changes. Most of the senior staff have been with the family for twenty years. The staff know loyalty is a strong family ethic and capability is very important.

Therefore when the second generation joined the business at senior levels they rarely posed any threat to non-family employees whose status was confined to supervisory levels. The management structures in a number of long-standing family businesses were based on traditional views that dictated positions of trust and authority were only accessible via blood or close kinship ties. However, by the time the third generation began to enter the business this assumption was being challenged. Developments both within the business communities and externally had created new working environments. Educational achievements and subsequent career opportunities amongst the third-generation Asians heralded the beginning of substantial upheaval for these family businesses. Greater access to higher education abroad meant the younger generation did not automatically expect to join the family business. Even in those cases where the family had great expectations on the younger generation to join the business they had to be prepared to face the loss of successors. This meant reconfiguring traditional attitudes towards management and recruiting from not only outside the family but also possibly outside their kin and even co-ethnic networks.

The growth and stabilisation of businesses created greater opportunities for non-family employees. These developments were accompanied by greater formalisation of management structures; in a number of cases experienced non-family staff were rewarded with senior management positions for their loyalty. The entry of the third generation subsequently created tensions as non-family employees perceived their entrance as a direct threat to the management positions they had achieved. The fears of non-family employees were justified, family ties meant that younger heirs would be fast-tracked into managerial positions;

> Amongst the other staff I could tell there was a feeling of questioning my credentials, they felt I was less qualified and experienced. Some probably felt the only reason I was there was because of who I was not what I can do. This was particularly from the senior staff who had been there a long time.

The entry of the third generation created a new experience for family business owners; they had to compromise with their workers rather than enforce changes to a submissive workforce. New entrants had to be guided into the business and find a way to build up their credibility with the workforce across all levels from senior management to those on the production line or shop floor. Older family members found ways to navigate the entrance of the younger generation through discussions and negotiations with their senior managers. This transition was not always smooth, there was a lot of stake personally and commercially for both generations of family members as well as for the non-family managers. The following respondent acknowledged the resentment of managers towards his promotion and described a difficult conflict with management:

> There were problems as my job was also a managerial role and the General Manager wasn't happy with my presence...The biggest problem I've faced within this company has been with the General Manager, initially after we clashed I left the company for a short time. In that time my father could see the General Manager wasn't helping the company and didn't renew his contract. I left because I felt maybe my perspective was wrong, but within a couple of months the organisation had changed completely and it was easier to rejoin. The concept of what the family wants from the business must be first and foremost at all times. I think the General Manager saw me as a threat and resented me because I was the son and so he treated me badly.

Across the cases there were small but important examples of how family members in senior position tried to reduce the gulf between themselves and non-family employees across all levels. This ranged from creating one large dining room that served everyone regardless of their status in the company, to lengthy discussions and negotiations with senior management focusing on the entry and roles of the younger generation. The entry of the younger generation was not as straightforward as it had once been; it was increasingly common practice to undergo a period of apprenticeship before admittance to senior management. The apprenticeship typically required the potential successors to spend a year working their way around the company being exposed to the full range of activities and processes across all levels of the organisation. This provided the younger generation with an opportunity to work their way through the organisation and understand the demands at different levels before moving into management positions and also minimised the likelihood of allegations that they did not have sufficient experience of the business to justify supervisory roles.

The final area of discussion in this section considers a new breed of successors that are unexpectedly emerging and having a significant impact on family firms – daughters. The previous section emphasised how the pool of successors had dramatically transformed across the generations. Family businesses had followed a strong tradition adopted by royalty and family businesses in other countries – succession was linear and male-dominated. This practice had created its own tensions for the Kenyan Asian family businesses during first- to second-generation transition when family members with sons were automatically elevated to superior positions compared with those who had only daughters. By the time the businesses were facing third-generation entry the profile of the successors had changed considerably. Not only were they more highly educated, with external professional overseas experience there was a slightly higher chance they would be female. The emphasis on education amongst the younger generation had not been limited to sons; in line with the Asian emphasis on education, daughters were encouraged as well. Of course there are differences in attitudes towards educating daughters across the different sub-groups within the Asian community (Janjuha-Jivraj and Mansukhani, 2002). The communities from which the cases are drawn highlight the obvious cyclical relationship between education and progress. Education forms the backbone of human capital that is particularly important for business development and this in turn provides a valuable resource for business development. Progression in turn creates more instances where members are encouraged to take advantage of educational opportunities.

There were very few businesses with daughters who joined the business. Where this occurred, their experiences have provided important insights into how family and non-family employees and other stakeholders reacted to their involvement in the business. Whilst the field of family business research is rich with studies on working dynamics of male family members, the same cannot be said of female involvement as work in this field is relatively sparse (Dumas, 1989, 1992; Matthews and Moser, 1998).

The involvement of other family members

The composition of families involved in businesses invariably meant brothers, uncles and cousins were drawn into the arena. The patterns of authority within these families often meant elder family members were venerated in accordance with the culture and customs of the community. This behaviour also had implications for the businesses as decisions were more likely to be made by committee, taking into account the desires and wishes of elder family members. Whilst this created greater opportunities to draw upon a wider pool of resources for the business, it also created problems particularly during times of inter-generational transition. One of the most common experiences described amongst the cases was the fallout of family members during the period of generational succession, in particular dissatisfaction about the choice of certain family members to lead the business. This type of conflict is not uncommon within family businesses, however the implications of these problems can be quite far-reaching within a tight-knit community. The Asian community in Kenya was one such example where family rifts had a knock-on effect not only disrupting the immediate and extended family networks but also extending to the wider co-ethnic community.

As one would expect, the families were initially reluctant to talk about family rifts that had plagued the businesses. However, when they did, certain trends emerged, which were repeated across the generations. For example, both second and third generations experienced tensions and resentment from other family members:

> My Uncles had been in the business since the beginning. I was the new boy and the first of my generation to join. My father was more sympathetic and had more understanding with me, but he didn't give in to me. My Uncles were resentful. I tried to grin and bear it because I was expected to respect my elders. This was the culture of our generation. We had to do things even if we didn't agree ... In the 1970s my Uncles left Kenya because of the political situation. They left myself and my father to run the business.

> When I joined the business it caused the first dispute between my father and my Uncles, they saw entrance with my father as threat. The tension grew and my Uncles went their separate ways. My father and grandfather agreed that the business should remain on one side of the family.

Similar examples were rife amongst the other cases and illustrate the tensions between family members concerned about the dilution of power with the entrance of the younger generation. Whilst it seems inevitable that family members would leave the business this had an unexpected effect on the business and even the ethnic community. The individuals who left the business took one of two routes, either they left the country or they started up on their own enterprise in Kenya. With the latter case this invariably meant creating a business in the same field they had previously been working in; it also meant they used the same contacts in terms of suppliers and possibly even marketed to the same customer base. This resulted in businesses operated by different strands of the same family competing aggressively with each other and eating into each other's market share, thereby destabilising the business and the family. In addition to the economic destruction there was also the emotional devastation as such behaviour deepened family rifts, which bled over into ethnic community and often deepened over successive generations.

Summary

The cases from Kenya illustrate a range of issues affecting families and businesses. The age of the businesses provides an important context when research conflicts and tensions between these bodies. A number of the issues that arose in the businesses were not necessarily ethnic-specific, however the implications of these problems and even the way in which solutions were generated often seemed to be representative of their culture and value systems. The experiences of family businesses that have survived the first round of inter-generational transition and are preparing for the next highlighted opportunities for business development. More of the respondents in these businesses talked about moving towards a split between ownership and management. Although this had not been implemented in the cases, discussions between the generations seemed to favour this approach as a way forward. The separation of ownership and management would enable the businesses to remain under family control but to be managed by external staff recruited for their skills and experience appropriate for the job. This also addressed the situation for the younger generation seeking their own career prospects away from the business as well as the more negative perceptions of nepotism in family firms.

5
South Asian Entrepreneurship in Britain – Push or Pull?

Introduction

Asian entrepreneurship in Britain is a combination of positive and negative forces affecting members of the community. South Asian entrepreneurship in Britain has its origins in the earlier settlers, from traders to peddlers. However, the influx of East African Asians in the late 1960s and early 1970s provided the bases for significant entrepreneurial activity. This chapter considers business activity within the British South Asian community. Beginning with a focus on the motivations for business start-up this provides an understanding of the founders' aspirations for the business. This in turn provides a base from which the development and dynamics of family businesses can be discussed. This chapter is split into two distinct areas beginning with a brief overview of theories surrounding entrepreneurial behaviour before focusing on issues specific to ethnic, and in particular Asian, entrepreneurship. The discussion focuses on an exploration of the 'Push and Pull' factors which facilitate the analysis of entrepreneurial behaviour within the migrant Asian community. This classification is commonly used to explore ethnic entrepreneurship (Ram and Jones, 1998) and enables the discussion to incorporate a wider range of issues from the various schools addressing entrepreneurship. Within this chapter areas relating to entrepreneurial behaviour introduced in Chapter 3 will be discussed further in the context of Asian business activity in Britain.

Business start-up

Analysis of entrepreneurial behaviour usually falls into one of two camps: individuals are either forced into business due to limited opportunities or are drawn into entrepreneurship based on positive associations and resources. A considerable body of research has been generated under each of these classifications, however the application of entrepreneurial behaviour is less clear-cut. Motivations often emerge from both the push and the pull camps in varying amounts. This discussion begins with a brief exploration of the push factors leading to entrepreneurship before moving on to the pull factors.

Push factors

Push factors are described as negative experiences that induce people to self-employment (Basu, 1999). The stimuli arise from a wide array of sources leading to gaps in perceived levels of satisfaction; they can range from basic needs for financial support and stability; not only for the individual, but also for the family and wider kinship circle. The psychological implications linked with the disparity between actual and perceived status provide a significantly strong stimuli to encourage entrepreneurship:

> Social marginality theory suggests that those in society who perceive a strong level of incongruence between their personal attributes and the role/s they hold will be motivated to change or reconstruct their social reality. (Stanworth *et al.*, 1989: 14)

The social marginality model has provided the foundations for a considerable body of research in the field of entrepreneurship (Kets de Vries, 1977; Stanworth *et al.*, 1989). This approach has also influenced the field of family business research, particularly when analysing the working dynamics of family members (Kets de Vries, 1993, 1996). In this context the social marginality model is used not only in the context of entrepreneurship but also as a means of understanding the implications on working dynamics between generations in family businesses. There is undoubtedly a clear link between the psychological motivations of entrepreneurs and how their subsequent behaviour influences the workings over family businesses. The founder's willingness to pass on the business is the most crucial factor affecting the succession process. The social marginality model argues the underlying motivations for business start-up are embedded in the individual's psyche, with significant emphasis on the need for autonomy and high internal locus of control. This builds on the work of Schumpeter (1934) who cited low self-esteem as an important stimulus for entrepreneurship, a process by which individuals could re-position themselves in society.

Such individuals are argued to be condemned to not only live in two different societies but also experience antagonistic cultures. However, this view was later criticised (cited by Ahmed, 1981) who argued the theory did not distinguish between individuals in a marginal situation or those with a marginal personality. This approach was derived from the view that an individual caught between two cultures did not always develop a marginal personality. However, it is the notion of a marginal personality that is described as a motivating factor in self-employment and underlies the social marginal theory. The critical factor in the social marginal model is how experiences of an individual result in entrepreneurial behaviour. The disparity between real and perceived levels of stability, and the subsequent imbalance in the physical and psychological aspects of a personality creates significant stimuli for entrepreneurship. Humans are unable to maintain a constant state of imbalance (Sites, 1990). Their need for a secure environment is overwhelming thereby reducing instability becomes paramount, thus creating an appropriate situation for entrepreneurship. The issue of marginality has been discussed in detail during this section as it provides an important basis, not only for business start-up amongst South Asian migrants, but also potentially affecting attitudes towards generational succession.

The stimuli for entrepreneurship does not mean that this activity will automatically yield positive results. The 'holy grail' in this debate has been attempts to unravel what factors constitute optimal conditions for realising entrepreneurial ambition. The background of an individual, their characteristics as well as their social capital need to combine to provide the ideal base for exploiting opportunities. The pull factors are as important as the push factors. The pull factors focus on resources available to individuals who are often argued to be embedded in strong culturalist traditions (Ram and Jones, 1998). It is for this reason pull factors are more easily identified amongst migrant communities that exhibit significant cohesion.

Pull factors

Pull factors refer to experiences at the other end of the spectrum; they are influences that are described as having a positive effect in encouraging entrepreneurship. This view rejects the notion of the labour market as negative and too simplistic because it cannot be applied to all experiences of business start-up. The pull factors are the intangible factors that cannot be measured financially or often by any other means. Whilst it would be reasonable to argue the push factors deal with the lower level needs of Maslow's hierarchy (1943) (i.e. the physical and survival needs), motivations within the pull factors are often embedded in the higher levels of the pyramid, social mobility, the use of personal skills and knowledge which may not be exploited through existing employment opportunities. It was highly probable that an entrepreneur was motivated by the highest level of Maslow's hierarchy (1943) – the need for self-actualisation. This desire for self-actualisation is described as a combination of personal creativity, philosophy as well opportunities within the environment.

Role models are a critical influence in the processes surrounding entrepreneurship. They may be derived from family members (immediate or extended) as well as close friends. Wider societal changes have encouraged greater recognition of entrepreneurs as role models by celebrating their successes. Reality, mingled with entrepreneurial myths resembling 'David and Goliath' accounts created legendary tails of entrepreneurship. The most influential role models are often cited as individual located in close proximity to the individual (Gibb, 1988; Stanworth *et al.*, 1989). Stanworth and Gray (1991) emphasised the influence of family members whereby certain 'entrepreneurial' characteristics are transmitted through the generations. In addition to family, informal networks provide an important source of role models and generation of social capital for entrepreneurial ventures. By their nature informal networks emerge and grow for a variety of sources, not solely limited to the business needs of members.

Changes in the wider environment over the last thirty years have led to a resurgence of small firm start-up and growth through greater encouragement of an enterprising culture by successive governments. Developments in the workplace such as increased flexibility and the phenomenal growth of sub-contracting work have created greater opportunities for part-time employees and freelance contractors (Stanworth and Gray, 1991). Furthermore, social attitudes have become more favourable towards self-employment as viable career alternatives. This cumulative effect has let to a more conducive environment for business start-up and support and in turn encouraged a more positive attitude towards entrepreneurship.

The final area of research to be discussed in this section is work collated under 'entrepreneurial traits' (Stanworth and Gray, 1991). Researchers in this area identified particular characteristics that were felt to influence the propensity of entrepreneurial behaviour amongst individuals, for example McClelland's (1961) theory on the need for achievement, nAch, as a considerable motivating force. Other researchers (Brockhaus, 1982; Caird, 1990; Chell *et al.*, 1991) argued that there was a close association between business start-up and the individual's need to control their environment (locus of control). Other areas include individual's risk-taking propensity (Carland *et al.*, 1984; Chell *et al.*, 1991), the need for independence (Bolton, 1971; Kets de Vries, 1977) and finally innovation and creativity (Moss Kanter, 1983). Economists argue entrepreneurs will pursue business goals in conditions of extreme uncertainty for the sake of financial rewards (Stanworth and Gray, 1991). However, it is the notion of uncertainty that generates considerable attention. McClelland (1961) argued risk-taking propensity amongst entrepreneurs is a calculated activity. This develops on Schumpeter's work (1934) where he argued that risk-taking was applicable to all business ownership rather than a defining factor of entrepreneurial behaviour.

The various approaches to identifying these traits has created a complex model of what constitutes entrepreneurial characteristics. However, Chell (1997) has been the primary force in identifying some of flaws of the approach. This has led to the development of the behavioural approach that argues entrepreneurial behaviour a specific process that is often context-specific (Gerber, 1995; Birley, 1996). This reinforces the notion of treating each entrepreneur as a separate entity rather than one group with similar characteristics. The behavioural approach helps researchers to understand how entrepreneurs operate in a particular manner, this is particularly important when considering succession, in attempting to understand motivations for encouraging or obstructing succession.

South Asian entrepreneurship in Britain

A report on ethnic minorities and labour market published in 2003 highlighted the trend of self-employment amongst specified South Asian groups (namely Indian and Pakistani) has consistently remained higher than their White counterparts (figures based on Labour Force Surveys 1998–2000). This trait was previously identified in the 1987 Labour Force Survey (Srinivasan, 1992). Such figures reinforce the popular myths about the Asian Midas touch (Khan, 1988). This in turn adds to the legend of Asians being culturally disposed to entrepreneurship, intensified by the fact that so many businesses are located in highly visible trades, such as retailing and catering (Rafiq, 1990).

By exploring the push and pull factors in relation to a specific ethnic group it is possible to draw out relevant influences and present more specific arguments on the workings of such businesses. Considerable work has focused on business start-up within ethnic communities that have a notable presence in the SME sector. For example, some researchers (Ward and Jenkins, 1984; Werbner, 1990; Srinivasan, 1992; Ram, 1994; Ram and Jones, 1998; Basu, 1999) represent a small proportion of the significant work on South Asian entrepreneurship in Britain. This research is an important contribution to the wider field of ethnic entrepreneurship, globally. Work on South Asian entrepreneurs in Britain is far more developed in terms of detailed analysis of sectors as well as subtle, but important differences between the sub-groups. This level of attention has generated work that identifies and focuses on the heterogeneous nature of the community.

South Asian push factors

As discussed in the previous section push factors refer to negative experiences that force entrance in entrepreneurship. The previous chapter discussed the experiences of the East African Asians and Indians during their migration to and settlement in the West. A lot of East African Asians had left behind successful businesses and the associated status within both their religious ethnic community and also the wider environment. The racism they experienced on entry into Britain undermined perceptions of security and stability for the migrants. This sudden and dramatic shift emphasised their precarious position, living in what Sites (1990) described as a continuous state of 'heightened fear'. This underpinned the socially marginal position of such groups and provided the stimulus for change (Ward and Jenkins, 1984) – a view supported by a number of researchers (Modood, 1992; Ballard and Hurst, 1994; Ram, 1994; Basu, 1999).

> there is a weighty body of evidence for the view that the Asian drive into self-employment is primarily a reaction against racism, blocked avenues of social mobility and wholesale job cuts, and a means of sheer survival. (Ram and Jones, 1998: 11)

Discrimination was argued to present a barrier to social mobility; this thesis was proposed by Boissevain *et al.* (1990) and developed by Srinivasan (1992). This theory incorporates the social marginality argument as an important rationale for Asian self-employment. As migrants experienced barriers to employment opportunities they sought to change their current status. Ward and Jenkins (1984), however, draw out criticisms with this theory. They argue businesses located in marginal sectors of the economy (as many visible Asian businesses have been – for example CTNs[1]) do not necessarily enable owners to engage in upward social mobility. Furthermore, many of these businesses were located in areas of high Asian settlement – ethnic enclaves (Auster and Aldrich, 1984). The developments of these settlements created markets for co-ethnic businesses. However, such businesses were largely life-style firms. The development of ethnic enclaves can be viewed as a double-edged sword. The most apparent and fundamental benefits of ethnic enclaves have been the abundant supply of labour supply and sources of various forms of capital (Light, 1972; Bonacich and Modell, 1980; Portes, 1998). However, ethnic enclaves create barriers to social and economic integration as well as exploitative labour practices within ethnic firms that many individuals tried to avoid in the mainstream (Sanders and Nee, 1987). This behaviour has been particularly characteristic of ethnic enclaves regardless of ethnic background or even geographical location. Portes (1981) argues working relationships within ethnic enclaves legitimise 'paternalistic work arrangements' justifying stricter working regimes and the lack of unionised activity.

The motivating force for the development of ethnic enclaves is the mobilizing of ethnic solidarity strengthened by experiences of migration and settlement. Over time, however, this momentum becomes difficult to maintain. In a number of cases the benefits of ethnic enclaves are temporary. Sanders and Nee (1987) highlighted socio-economic advantages for Chinese and Cuban immigrants who had broken out of their embedded networks. The profiles of these individuals were largely similar to non-Hispanic white immigrants (in terms of educational achievement and occupation). From this finding it is reasonable to argue that businesses need to move away from resources that are predominantly based on embedded networks in order to have a greater chance of survival. This concept of 'breakout' (Ram and Hillin, 1994) is advocated for business survival (Waldinger *et al.*, 1990). The concept of 'breakout' is the process whereby businesses move from the marginal ethnic segments towards mainstream markets within the economy, not only improving survival rates but also enabling the owner and family to achieve a level of social integration and mobility.

Ethnic cohesion experienced by the migrant Asian community reinforced the importance of repayment. Whilst Portes (1998) emphasises the notion of reciprocity is inextricably linked to status within the ethnic community, he also highlights the importance of approval from amongst the group. The peer pressure exerted by the ethnic community can be so great that financial loans can be made on the basis of implicit trust towards other members. Portes (1998) argues that trust within these relationships is paramount because obligation is enforceable through the informal power exerted by the community rather than relying on legal frameworks. The benefits of shared resources have already been discussed in this section, however the above scenario creates its own set of problems. In certain cases it is likely that members were coerced into supporting fellow members, perhaps to repay a debt generated in East Africa. The experiences of migration may have made the ability to repay the debt difficult, however status and implicit community pressure would make it equally difficult for the donor not to provide support through one means or another. A further important result of greater community cohesion has been the emergence of business role models, usually in the form of fathers, uncles and other close male relatives or friends. As business ownership and status are intertwined within ethnic networks, it is only inevitable that many business owners also become elevated to the position of role model. Furthermore, in the South Asian community, entrepreneurship has long been perceived as desirable, particularly in the absence of skilled employment opportunities:

> Working for someone else is worth nothing. It is of no use. You work and you have nothing to show for it. But in self-employment, if you work hard enough you get results – you can make something of your life... Self-employment, whatever the scale of the business had a certain prestige attached to it. (Srinivasan, 1992: 66–71)

Ethnic solidarity provided a means by which families could maintain a tight control over the younger generation. Experiences where the younger generation had witnessed an increased constant income and greater status elevation led to family businesses that were likely to become a breeding ground for entrepreneurs (Ram and Jones, 1998). At the other extreme where the younger generation had experienced racism either themselves or through their family, especially from customers, it deterred them from self-employment (Chan and Janjuha-Jivraj, 2000).

A commonly cited aspect of ethnic entrepreneurship is the reliance on family members as sources of labour. Research surrounding familial involvement in ethnic businesses provided the businesses with a unique labour resource that enabled them to flourish. However, some researchers feel familial involvement in the business can be over-emphasised in the stories of business start-up and success. For example, Jones *et al.* (1993) argue that family involvement in business is not necessarily a distinct ethnic characteristic but rather an inherent response to the disadvantages of SMEs. Whilst the author acknowledges this contribution, work on ethnic solidarity argues that families play a pivotal role in the development and maintenance of strong community ties. Sanders and Nee (1987) develop on Weber's (1978 [1922]) work where he characterised the high degree of solidarity within the family unit as 'household communism':

> Both the qualities of solidarity and communism become valuable social capital in facing the uncertainties and challenges of adaptation to a new society. The strength of family boned may also allow kinship ties to be used for economic adaptation. Particularly in the case of immigrants who initiate small businesses, the family household provides essential unpaid labour for thinly capitalized businesses to start up and compete. (Sanders and Nee, 1987: 765)

In his exploration of social capital, Portes (1998) explores the impact of bounded solidarity as a form of social control within groups, this has already been discussed within the context of ethnic networks. This section considers social capital as a source of family support. Citing work by Coleman (1993), Portes (1998) describes the nature of social capital as it flows from parent to child. This exchange creates and reinforces the notion of filial obligation. Furthermore, this context of social capital also enforced social control, not only within the family but even as the family unit is presented within the tightly-knit ethnic community. Through this behaviour elder members of the extended family as well as other older community members all participate in rearing the younger generation. Parallels can be drawn with Gold's (1995) work on parental roles among Israeli immigrant families in the United States, where the community assumes responsibility for the development and growth of younger members.

Marger (2001) argues social capital plays a particularly important role amongst migrant families. Decisions for migration are based on parental willingness to seek an improved life to provide a better life for their children. This argument is developed on the premise that individuals voluntarily leave a successful business. For the Ugandan Asians this was not the case, however it is an argument that can be applied to the experiences of Asians from the other East African countries. Marger's (2001) work focused on the experiences of ethnic groups migrating to Canada, and he concluded the motivations to migration for his sample indicated that amongst the migrant community, social capital did not lie in their own ethnic group, but rather the broader society. This conclusion was based on migrants' expectations about their future settlement and better socio-economic conditions for the next generation. This argument provides a positive approach to the experience of migrants and their reliance on social capital. Sanders and Nee (1987) cite Park and Burgess (1921) who argued that assimilation eventually reduced the reliance on ethnic solidarity. The author would argue integration is a more reasonable and desirable outcome rather than assimilation, but this nevertheless reduces the need for ethnic solidarity. As the next generation grow and achieve greater integration, according to Marger (2001), Park and Burgess (1921) they build on the social capital from a wider range of ethnic sources, rather than sole reliance on their embedded ethnic networks.

Whilst this is acknowledged by the author, the nature of family relations within the workplace are likely to be accentuated as a result of ethnic background. The impact of social capital available to ethnic entrepreneurs meant that businesses had a ready supply of labour. Family members provided a crucial aspect of this labour supply, they were willing to undertake unfavourable working conditions for the greater good of the family. As many Asian businesses were built around the culture and traditions of the owner (typically the father) the organisational structure of many businesses was largely patriarchal. The impact of social capital amongst families meant that within ethnic groups there was a greater expectation for the younger generation to pitch in and support the needs of the growing business:

> '... those of Chinese and Asian descent have more hierarchically organised families and a clearer sense of family loyalty and joint responsibility'.
> (Boissevain et al., 1990: 134)

The initial involvement of children within ethnic businesses was not necessarily a precursor for family business succession, however their involvement was seen to reinforce cultural trends and values that had constituted important customs within the Indian culture. Basu (2000) highlights this argument citing work by Smith (1993) who emphasised the importance of close interrelationships between the family and the business, particularly within the Hindu community:

> '... the custom of keeping the business close to domestic life was adhered to for a large part of the eighteenth century by family firms in India'. (Basu, 2000: 6)

This supports earlier work by Werbner (1981), who emphasised the importance of total household contribution and a 'Protestant work ethic' as characterising the Pakistani ethos. Often this degree of long-term loyalty is only achieved through blood ties, however Ram and Holliday (1993) argue this involvement is a critical factor in the success of businesses, particularly during start-up or major growth periods (periods when the businesses require greater resource investments). The belief in the benefits of family involvement is so strong that Bjerke (1998) argues families are the bedrock of businesses. Ram (1994) not only acknowledges the strength of family involvement in ethnic businesses, but also argues for the negative consequences of over-reliance on familial resources, which can potentially stunt business growth. This view generates the need to consider the quality of resources drawn from the family, for example in terms of educational and professional experience, particularly when considering heirs for family business succession. This will be considered in greater detail in the next chapter.

As previously discussed, Asian family businesses are likely to reinforce a strong patriarchal culture. The involvement of the younger generation has been introduced and will be discussed in greater detail in subsequent chapters. One other family member however plays a critical role in the start-up and survival of the business – the wife (or partner) of the founder. Work on women in ethnic businesses has highlighted women as maintaining a crucial yet invisible role within the business (Ram and Holliday, 1993; Dhaliwal, 1998). The common theme amongst these pieces of research is the exploitation and sub-ordination of women who are the 'real resource' and 'critical' to business success. The source of this behaviour is argued to lie in the founder's overriding beliefs and attitudes. This will be explored further in the next chapter.

Assessment of the debate on Asian entrepreneurship

This chapter has presented a discussion of the different research on entrepreneurship, focusing on ethnic (Asian) business start-up. The push/pull typology was used to present balanced arguments describing experiences leading to business start-up. In the section on Asian start-up, the push factors dealt with the social marginal theory resulting from discrimination experienced by migrants and perceived gaps between their actual and ideal status. The arguments centred around the notion that rather than possessing the skills or experience that made Asians predisposed to entrepreneurship, entrance into self-employment was the result of frustration and the need to find ways to navigate the blocked social mobility status. The pull factors on the other hand explored what

Ram and Jones (1998) describe as the 'culturalist tradition', the ability of ethnic migrants to draw upon their social capital from within the embedded ethnic networks. The form of this capital varies, but can include access to financial resources, co-ethnic and family labour, contacts that may generate customers or suppliers and shared experiences of start-up, particularly in low knowledge-intensive sectors. Whilst it is acknowledged that long-term involvement in ethnic enclaves or over-reliance on ethnic or family resources can stifle business growth, the benefits are considerable and particularly important as businesses struggle through the initial precarious stages of start-up and the growth corridor.

Social capital of ethnic migrants provides an important means of accessing resources, enabling individuals to establish competitive businesses. The range of capital available (including previous business experience and positive cultural attitudes) enables individuals to develop businesses in an atmosphere that is conducive to encouraging entrepreneurship. There are however limitations as the risks associated with business start-up are high. For the migrant community entrepreneurship often provided the only route through which individuals could navigate their way out of blocked social mobility. Therefore, amongst the migrant community business start-up was often the result of 'push' factors notably discrimination both socially and economically. This in turn reinforced the social marginality notion and provided the initial impetus for business start-up. For many of these individuals self-employment presented a means of achieving social mobility. Through their improved status individuals had the opportunity to reclaim the former glory they had experienced in East Africa and reach a higher platform from which they could achieve a better quality of life for their children.

It is far too simplistic, however, to argue that the experiences of business start-up for the migrant community were due to push *or* pull factors. Both categories work together to provide an explanation of the phenomena of Asian business start-up. For example, ethnic solidarity was the result of migration and discriminatory experiences. Self-employment, which was a reaction to discrimination, was more accessible due to the social capital of migrants. As larger numbers of individuals established their businesses they provided a form of chain migration for successive community members and also became recognised as role models inspiring subsequent migrants to achieve success through entrepreneurship. This process has continually been repeated many times over the last thirty years. There are also other socio-economic factors that influence entrepreneurship; Light (1984) highlighted education and class position of migrants as key determinants. The educational attainment of migrants or their previous business experience (prior to migration) influenced the likelihood of entrepreneurship and longer-term success. These individuals were likely to be more flexible and have the ability to develop necessary managerial and inter-personal skills as well as the ability to confidently negotiate transactions with the wider business community. Previous discussions in this book have highlighted the educational and professional differences amongst the various Asian sub-groups and this in turn explains why certain groups have higher degrees of sustained entrepreneurial success than others. Therefore, these factors also provide important contribution in understanding the experience and reasons for significant Asian business start-up.

This assessment of Asian business start-up will need to be modified, perhaps quite significantly, as future work focuses on the experiences of younger generation entrepreneurship. These are individuals who have achieved greater integration with the wider community, received a Western education and have a range of professions and business opportunities available to them. Yet the social capital available to the younger generation has also undergone radical changes and these factors need investigation through further research.

Note

1. CTNs – Confectioners, Tobacconists and Newsagents.

6
Working Dynamics in British Asian Family Firms

Introduction

As family firms traverse both professional and personal spheres of individuals involved in the business, the dynamics of family members are inevitably influenced by a wide range of factors. The community-contextualised family business model (Figure 4.2) represents the range of individuals who have significant influences in the dynamics of family firms. Within this context certain factors inevitably have a more profound influence on dynamics from the onset, notably the entrance of the younger generation and reactions of other family members. The research area of working dynamics in family firms has focused predominantly on control and power. For example exploring how incumbent family members prepare for the potential loss of control within their business, both emotionally and practically. This has a critical impact on the working relationships between the founder and the successor. Furthermore, the entry route for the younger generation is an important factor that influences the nature of subsequent working relations. The first section in this chapter explores how obligation manifests itself in business entry, both through filial and parental forms of obligation. As discussed previously the mode of entry of the younger generation into the business presents a critical basis for future working relations. The discussion will explore how the mode of entry affects generational dynamics. The next section considers the impact of 'other' family members in the business, namely mothers. Their role in the family business can vary considerably and have wide-ranging effects on how they influence working dynamics of 'active' family members.

Obligation

The transfer of ownership in a family business is more than a straight-forward business transaction for all sides involved and indeed other parties associated with the family and the business. This process is often deeply emotional. Whilst one person is relinquishing control, associated forms of power and even social status, the incoming successor has to contend with establishing their own identity on the business. This often entails working within the difficult constraints of an environment where staff remain loyal 'old guard' (Achua, 1997). These emotional tensions inevitably become intensified as both generations have to manage their personal relationship with one another. The father (and founder) has to deal with his limitations within the business environment. For many individuals who have spent their lives building up business empires, transfer of ownership and control is the harshest reminder of their mortality (Kuratko, 1995). At the same time the younger generation has to precariously manage the balance of their desires to move the business forward and mould it according to their personality and experiences whilst also respecting the traditions and challenges of their father.

The conditions cited above illustrate how business entry of the younger generation is not usually a straightforward affair. Whilst a number of family businesses groomed the younger generation for business entry, the entry routes the younger generation ended up taking were quite different from what was expected. Obligation plays a significant role in the entrance of the younger generation. Amongst ethnic families and communities where there is a great deal of social capital, obligation was inevitably a precursor to business involvement. This is evident in the research focusing on ethnic migrant businesses and often manifested through informal involvement providing critical business support (Werbner, 1990; Ram, 1994; Mattausch, 1998). Indeed the propensity to rely on co-ethnic members to develop competitive business practices was noticeably higher within the South Asian business community (Soar, 1991; Jones and Rose, 1993; Ram and Holiday, 1993). In most cases the business networks developed around the personal networks of entrepreneurs, building on their social capital to generate mutually beneficial relationships satisfying a combination of business and social needs. Over an extended period, members of community accepted this form of social capital as inherent to the fabric of their networks and this was even greater within families. The cultural norms embedded in this behaviour created the basis for repetition of such practices (Adler and Kwon, 2002) and in particular reinforced the notion of obligation as a common theme within families and communities.

Obligation as stimuli for entry into the family business can fall into one of two classifications: 'filial' obligation – the most common form whereby families have expectations on the younger generation to join the business. In these cases the younger generation are 'groomed' for their role in the business from a young age. This form of obligation was very common in the Kenyan cases discussed in the previous chapters. An opposite, yet equally powerful form of entry is achieved through 'parental' obligation, whereby pressure is placed on the parents to allow their children to enter the business. This occurs in situations where the parents have not made provision for the younger generation to join the business nor had any expectations of the need to admit their children into the business. The presence of either forms of obligation and how both generations respond have a considerable influence on subsequent working and personal relationships among family members and other stakeholders, such as non-family employees, clients, business partners and even customers. This discussion considers how these different forms of obligation impact the dynamics of family members in these cases. Obligation for business entry can be further subdivided into anticipated and unanticipated triggers. The difference between the two classifications is simply where there were expectations among family for the younger generation to join the business (anticipated). The opposite is the case for unanticipated obligation, instances where there were no expectations for the younger generation to join the business.

Filial obligation – 'Anticipated' triggers

Increased educational achievement amongst ethnic communities along with a wider range of opportunities in the professional market led many commentators to speculate family businesses, and in particular those of South Asian origin, would face a demise. Figures drawn from the 2001 Census show that self-employment activity varies across the British South Asian community (National Statistics, 2005). People from Pakistan (23%) (along with Chinese) are more likely to be self-employed compared to other ethnic groups, 13 per cent of Indians are self-employed. These statistics do indicate a shift towards professions amongst Indians and other South Asian communities; however, the family business community still represents a vibrant component of the economy.

Parental attitudes towards younger generation entry in the British cases were not uniform. However, in the majority of the cases, older family members *did have* expectations for younger generation entry into the business. From a young age the children were groomed to become successors of the founders. This often created a formidable sense of responsibility amongst the younger generation. The aspirations of the younger generation created a potential conflict, whilst they had developed their personal ambitions for future careers they did not pursue them deferring to the family's wishes. However when asked about business entry they felt this was *their own decision*, whilst also acknowledging explicit family desires for them to join the business. There were instances where the personal career desires of the younger generation were very strong but even in these cases they yielded to the family's will:

> I had not initially expected to join the family business. My father hoped I would join the business, but he wouldn't pressurise us to join, but we [respondent and brother] saw that our father thought it would be ideal if we joined the business. By joining the business I would be able to continue my father's hard work.

The mixed signals in the above quote can be contrasted with the clear and specific views of his father:

> It was my plan that [my son] would finish his education and join me in the business. That way we were able to expand [the business].

Whilst this respondent had plans for his own career as a pilot, his parents ignored this by encouraging him to study Management at university, as they felt this would be beneficial to the family business. During the interview the father did not acknowledge the personal ambitions of his son. Instead he was very persistent in assuming his son (who was also the eldest of two boys) had wanted to join the business, as would be the case with the younger son on the completion of his education.

The attitude of the older generation in the above quotes is symbolic of a very traditional patriarchal culture which has strong resonance in many sectors of the South Asian community. Within these value systems collective family welfare is prioritised over personal desires with decisions often made by the father as the head of the family. The above quotes show the older generation only considered options for the younger generation that were aligned with their views (i.e. the entrance of his son into the business). If the father were to accept or even acknowledge the alternative views expressed by his son this would challenge the norms that establish the framework both within the family and the business. However, the son viewed his entrance as his *personal choice* to join and help his father. In a subtle manner he acknowledged that he had made personal sacrifices for the greater good of the business and the family. This case shows a dramatic imbalance of power between the two generations and the subsequent ambiguity between personal perceptions of both respondents. For the son to accept this position and live without conflict in the family and work within the family, he had to alter his perceptions, in that he helped his father *rather* than being forced by his parents to join the business. This enabled the younger generation to attempt to regain some feeling of control over their life and future.

Other cases were less drastic but still displayed a strong patriarchal dynamic in the relationship. This had an overwhelming influence on the entry of the younger generation. In these cases the younger generation exhibited a greater willingness to join the business and had remained fairly flexible on their personal career ambitions. This influenced their approach to higher education and choice of university degree. The younger respondents did not discuss the possibility of rebelling against parental wishes, on the contrary, their responses showed they felt content with fulfilling parental expectations, as this would please their parents and this was what any child would do. These cases represent filial obligation in its most pure form:

> With the degree I chose I had flexibility. I had always expected to go into the family business, but if I had done a Law degree I may have gone into Law. The problem was the time commitment.

> I knew I would always join the business, it was just a matter of when I would join. I went to work for a firm for a couple of years, but the business was growing and my father needed more help. My brother was still at university and so I joined the business.

In these cases both of the respondents were clear about filial expectations upon them and this had a direct influence over their approaches to higher education. Even when the younger generation worked in external companies their longer-term goals were to join the business. It is inevitable that in these cases the younger generation was subjected to a certain amount of emotional pressure, either consciously or subconsciously, in order for them to adhere to familial expectations. Having been groomed to join the business from a young age these individuals seemed to be quite subdued and in some ways detached from decisions they were making about their futures and career choices. This behaviour continued after entry into the family business. In many ways this would be expected and possibly even supported by fathers with strong personalities. These dynamics fitted in the strong father – weak son typology (Dyer and Handler, 1994). Whilst this dynamic occurs across a range of family firms, the emphasis on veneration of older family members means this behavioural pattern is more likely to occur. This supports research by Werbner (1981) and Boissevain *et al.* (1990) who argued that Asian families had strong ties of loyalty and hence obligation. These factors have a considerable impact on wider family involvement in the business – often highlighted by traits of deferred personal gratification for the greater good of the family and a long-term commitment to business.

In these cases the relationship between the two generations was relatively top-heavy although quite subtle and it was difficult to distinguish if there was any resentment or regret amongst the younger generation. The attitude across these cases implied that the younger generation took a natural course of action that was to be expected. They felt in their own way they had a choice, but they had chosen what their family wanted. None of the respondents described their situation as having been forced into that position.

> I encouraged both my children to get involved in the business. Deep down I knew that [my son] would join ... Whatever [my son] wanted to do I would have supported him, but I was very pleased when he joined the business.

These cases illustrate how the younger generation joined the business through 'anticipated' obligation. In these top-heavy relationships it was evident that the father was the key decision-maker and had the greatest influence in their relationship. The control of power was evident from the initial entrance of the younger generation to the business. In a number of instances the father determined the role of the younger generation and in turn dictated whom they were exposed to within the business, over time the older respondents felt they were able to delegate more responsibility to the younger generation and so achieve a better balance. The older respondents were still keen to maintain control over the business by retaining their position as ultimate decision-makers. This was a view often reinforced by members of the younger generation, they were perfectly comfortable with their fathers retaining significant business responsibility. This behaviour arises from a combination of factors, namely the relative youth and inexperience of the younger generation. However, reverting to the father–son dynamics these cases clearly illustrate another facet to the top-heavy relationship, the compliance of the younger generation into the business set a precedent for the working relationship. The younger respondents knew their entrance into the business was critical for its continuation. In a number of cases the businesses had been established with the expectation that the younger generation would take on the business and continue this legacy. Therefore amongst the younger generation their entry was not considered to be the result of obligation or pressure that had forced them into an undesirable situation, instead it was accepted as their responsibility within the family.

Filial obligation – 'Unanticipated' triggers

Filial obligation arising from unanticipated triggers emerged when sudden events occurred within the family or business, prompting younger generation entry into the business. In these cases there had been no prior expectations on the younger generation to join the business. These businesses had been established solely to provide a base for family stability. The younger generation were expected to develop their own careers upon the completion of their University degrees. Two cases from the sample of British respondents experienced this scenario as a trigger for business entry. In these cases the younger generation had embarked on their own career paths that were distinct from the family business. However in both cases familial emergencies resulted in the younger respondents moving away from their careers to support the family business. In these cases the younger generation considered their move into the family business as a short-term measure until the problems were resolved. Over time, however, the cases required the continued involvement of younger family members. This was an important factor when analysing the ensuing working relationship that developed between the generations.

In one case study (B1, Appendix 2) the parents had been adamant that the son would not join the business and instead carve out his own career path following the successful completion of his studies. However, as the mother had become ill she was no longer able to remain active in the business. The situation was further compounded by the nature of her illness requiring her husband to spend considerable time away from the business to look after her. Only one family member remained in the business, the father's cousin, who was unable to manage the business on his own. This led to the son deciding to leave his job in the city and work in the business as stopgap (for twelve months) until the father could resume his position. However, this temporary position extended beyond the initial twelve-month period well into the second year:

> It was my choice, the business was restructuring and needed the manpower. Initially the plan was to spend one year in the business and then return to the city to take up a job with one of the banks that had offered me a place ... When I joined the business the primary aim was to make sure the business survived for the next twelve months. Over time and with analysis we realised the market for ethnic foods was a good market and so we shifted our target and developed a five-year plan.

The younger respondent still wanted to resume his own career at some point in the future, however this was constantly challenged by the future prospects of the business. He was very aware of his responsibilities particularly reinforced as he was the only child and although other family members were beneficiaries of the business none of them had expressed any desire to join the business. The older respondent in this case presented an equally diplomatic view to the longer-term involvement of his son. He had not intended his son to join the business; however, he acknowledged his son's entrance enabled the business to remain in family ownership and management:

> I didn't influence [my son] to join the business, it was his own decision to join. I didn't want to force my son to do anything, he chose what degree subject to study ... When the business split, [my son] joined for a year because I needed him. But he kept his options open, so he could go back to his job if he wanted to pursue his career path. I was pleased [my son] had settled down, but I was worried that he would feel he was missing out on what his fellow students had ... opportunities to keep up and network with others.

The dynamic of the second generation in these cases was not as top-heavy as the previous examples. The relationship that developed in this case study was far more equal and derived from mutual respect. Both the father and the son valued their relationship, both personally and professionally, leading to greater communication about all aspects of the business. The nature of this relationship meant the son had greater flexibility to question and even challenge his father in business decisions. This was something other family members found difficult to accept. In particular the father described his wife's discomfort at the openness in their relationship:

> I think it helps that I accept my son as a colleague rather than as a son. My wife finds it difficult to understand my relationship with him, she doesn't understand why he argues with me, she feels sons shouldn't argue with their fathers.

The father–son working relationship in this case was a stark contrast to antagonistic and competitive father–son relationships described earlier that are very prolific in the family business field (Levinson, 1971; Kets de Vries, 1996). Once again the circumstances that triggered the entry of the younger generation provided an important factor in the ensuing relationship between the father and the son. The older respondent was aware of the sacrifices his son had made for the sake of the business. The father, therefore, nurtured the working relationship to empower his son and create a rewarding experience. This may well have been the father's motivation to compensate to the younger generation with more delegation. There was also a greater willingness to handover control at a much faster rate than the previous cases. Although the founder will have had strong attachments towards the business, the extent of his gratitude to the younger generation and also guilt led to an emotional detachment from the business.

In cases like this the events leading to the entry of the younger generation create a split in relationship between the founder and the business. As entrepreneurs establish businesses their identity becomes intertwined with the business to the extent they lose sight of their own mortality. Researchers in the field of family businesses have acknowledged the entry of the younger generation often heralds recognition of an individual's mortality (Kuratko, 1995). This readjustment creates tensions between the generations and is often the underlying reason for the antagonistic relationship between father and son. In cases of unanticipated 'filial' obligation the unexpected entry of the younger generation and associated events force the older generation to recognise their limitations as an individual. Through this realisation the attitudes of the older generation towards the business and their own immortality undergo radical changes. Whilst expected filial obligation discussed earlier led to a top-heavy relationship, unexpected filial obligation is likely to develop a more balanced dynamic between both generations.

As briefly mentioned this form of entry led to a more balanced working relationship and was appreciated by both generations, there were other family members who found this difficult to accept, as illustrated earlier by the mother's reaction. A more balanced working relationship was not culturally synchronised with Asian traditions and this created further tensions for older family members. The father of the founder was an active force in the business, albeit based in India, who had regular contact and input into the business. The founder felt he was in a position of having to balance two very different relationships, that with his father and with his son, and also very different expectations each had for the business. The relative freedom of control he had given to his son was completely disparate to the top-heavy relationship he still had with his father:

> Sometimes it's very difficult, I understand the ideas and direction my son wants to go with the business. I can't stand in his way, in principle we both agree on a direction and then work on the finer details. But at the same time my own father, although he is in India he still gives an input about his views on the business, which are not always the same as my son. So I have to keep both of them happy, this isn't easy.

The situation of the founder is likely to be more particular to family businesses in the Asian community. The dynamics in Asian family businesses are heavily influenced by the veneration of elder members. Experiences of migration and settlement in the West reinforced cultural traits and values through reinforced kinship solidarity and through the notion of household communism. Hiro (1991) defines the distinction between older and younger family members:

> Age is a mark of wisdom; youth a mark of inexperience ... The head of the family has authority over other members of it, even those who are married and are themselves fathers. (1991: 7)

Through this behaviour certain aspects of the culture were reinforced far more than perhaps they would have been had the families remained in their countries of origin. In these cases emphasis on traditional values of the household as a unit was so revered that family members were committed to protecting its sanctity. The practice of extended families living under one household was very common amongst first-generation migrants and more importantly it provided a significant source of social capital for the development and sustainability of family businesses. Extended families living in one house provided a means for older members to protect their younger, more vulnerable family members from undesirable influences of the West. This shroud of protection also extended to wives who were often discouraged from working outside the ethnic community. The emphasis on familial attitudes was reinforced by the common practice of extended families living together. This may have been a by-product of discriminatory housing practices, but for many migrants it was an important aspect of their culture they were keen to maintain. In other cases the sons would move away once they had got married, but all the properties remained under joint ownership of all the male members in the family. These living arrangements encouraged the patriarchal tradition of the Asian culture. Despite their socio-economic development, sons still deferred to the demands of their fathers or elder male relatives. Research by Goodwin and Cramer (1997) on extended families has found this is a declining practice; however, the roots of this practice reinforced the hierarchical position of elder family members that has infiltrated, survived and impacted family businesses.

Parental obligation

Parental obligation is located at the other end of the younger-generation business entry spectrum. This classification arose when the younger generation 'forced' their way into the business against the wishes of their parents. The incidences of this were surprisingly high amongst the cases. In these situations as with unexpected filial obligation there were no expectations on the younger generation to join the business, instead the parents had encouraged the children to complete their university education and develop their own careers.

In one case (B2, Appendix 2) the younger respondent had started university with a view to graduating before embarking on his career in dentistry. He completed two years before deciding to withdraw from his course and join the family business. The entrance of the younger generation created a difficult situation for the family. The father had suffered a series of personal traumas through family ill health and bereavement over the previous ten years. His intention was to wind down his business activity through selling the business and retiring to India. The father had already begun to implement this plan by divesting units in the business. The son was struggling with his choice of degree and unmotivated to continue his studies, his desire was to join the business. The father was caught in a difficult position, he had already started downsizing the business and he also felt the son was not mature enough to handle a business. After a great deal of persuasion from the son the father gave him a job within the business. The task allocated to the son was very demanding and the father hoped this would discourage the son from wanting to remain in the business and instead return to complete his degree. To the surprise of the father and the rest of the family the son successfully managed the unit he was running and against the odds generated a profit. Once the father made the decision to keep his son in the business new strategies needed to be implemented to enable the business to grow in order to provide a strong base for the son. This situation created another source of tension, the father was forced to put his own retirement plans on hold in order to support his son in the business. The father worked on the business developing its growth and expanding it rapidly with a view to long-term floatation.

The relationship between father and son was already quite fraught and the impact of the son forcing his way into the business created further tension and resentment. The father had set the son up in a position where he expected failure, but the son proved him wrong. Whilst the father wanted to provide for his son, he was angry and resentful that the son had forced his way into the business:

> No, I didn't want [my son] to join the business. I wanted him to stand on his own feet, with his profession...I'm still not happy about him joining the business, I don't think it was the right thing for him...he [son] decided to enter the business when it wasn't very big. I had made my retirement plans but this had to change, [my son] took this from me. I wanted to retire in India with an income. Instead I have had to be proactive in developing the business. This expansion has forced me to stay in the UK longer than I wanted. He forced me to give him things rather than me giving by affection. [My son] got too much too soon.

The son was aware of the father's hostility and the influence it had on both their working and personal relationships, for example whilst at work the son would try to avoid directly approaching his father if he had a problem, instead he would go to his uncle. In doing so the son did not have to expose his weaknesses to his father. He was aware of the problems within their relationship and described their personal relationship as strained.

Another case in this category had similar experiences leading to the younger generation entering the business. In this second case the younger generation had enrolled on a number of computing courses after completing his 'A' levels but he did not pursue them. Instead his desire was to join the family business as soon as possible:

> After my 'A' Levels I had different jobs, I worked in a hotel, a restaurant and a pizza place. These were all short-term jobs. Then in 1983 I started to work for my father in the news agency. My dad didn't really want me to join the business, but I persisted and he let me get involved... My father had bought a second unit and he was finding it difficult to manage both places, so I joined him to help him manage it. This was meant to be as a temporary measure, but I stayed on and we developed the business.

As with the previous case the father in this case had established the business as a means of providing support for the family during the education of the children. The business was not considered sufficient to warrant the entrance of another family member and so once the younger generation was on board both generations focused on transforming the business into a large food manufacturing business with retail outlets across London. Although the father initially was not happy with the son's determination to join the business, he finally accepted the son's decision, enabling both generations to work well together. However, the son was conscious that there were family members who still did not approve of his decision to join the business:

> They didn't want me to come into the business, they were worried the prospects weren't very promising. Now they are happy. But my uncle and aunty were adamant that I should have carried on studying, they were very critical about my decision and only backed down in 1995, after we had turned the business around.

In both of these cases the older generation displayed parental obligation by accepting the younger generation into the business despite their reluctance. The outcomes across these two cases contrast sharply between the strained resentful relationship in the former case and the positive rapport that developed in the latter. In case B2 both parties were aware of the negative feelings towards each other, whilst they worked hard to achieve an adequate working relationship, past experiences shaped a failing personal relationship, with severe long-term consequences. In this case both respondents acknowledged the father was responsible for decisions, regarding investments and long-term strategies for the business. Although 'involved', both respondents described this involvement as limited and largely cosmetic. The physical working environment reinforced this; the head office housed the respondent and his brother-in-law, whilst the son's office was situated an hour away in one of the units. This case was the exception where both generations did not share the same business premises. Whether or not this was a conscious decision the physical distance of the offices redefined the cleft between the two generations and it reinforced the superior position of the father.

The mother – The silent buffer

The community-contextualised family business model (Figure 4.2) emphasises the overlap between family members, the business and the entrepreneur. Business transition of family firms is not limited solely to the retiring founder and heir. Family businesses by their very nature, both influence and are influenced by additional family members (Mars and Ward, 1984; Dyer and Handler, 1994). Family involvement within a business can be split between individuals who are actively involved in the business and those who are not. Active family members work in the business on a regular basis and work towards a long-term aim of eventually taking over control of the business. Non-active family members have no or sporadic involvement with the business, they are likely to be involved in their own personal careers. Yet non-active family members may still have an input on decisions made regarding the business, which may affect long-term strategies adopted. This discussion focuses on one member in particular, the mother[1] and her influence during inter-generational transition.

The literature on family firms highlights familial labour as a crucial resource for such businesses (Baines and Wheelock, 1998); however, most of the research emphasises this as a predominantly ethnic resource (Ram and Holliday, 1993; Phizaclea and Ram, 1996). Existing work on family business dynamics explore the impact of partnerships or sibling rivalry (Marshack, 1994) but very little attention has been paid to the involvement of the mother during generational transition. This may be attributed to the traditional polarised approach adopted in the field of family business that divides the family and business. However, an additional reason for the lack of emphasis on her involvement may be simply due to the fact that the role of non-active family members is often overlooked in research. This discussion, therefore, represents a significant step towards understanding the role of the mother not only during succession but also as a force influencing dynamics and relations in family firms.

In most cases the mother's role was described as very limited often with no specific role. In other cases the active family members described the mothers as having involvement in the business at any stage. Whilst it is arguable these mothers had no active involvement in the cases if one were to assume they helped during its initial start-up and development the following observations can be made – the fathers in these cases were very strong figures both within the business and the family. Attitudes towards the mother reinforced the traditional patriarchal image of the father within Asian businesses. As one would expect these founders would not acknowledge support from anyone, particularly female family members. Over time the founder either ignored or chose to forget the involvement of his wife within the business. The influence of the founder on the younger generation is illustrated by the latter's responses as they categorise their mothers in the same role. This may either be because the younger generation was not aware of the involvement of the mother, especially if it was behind the scenes, or the younger generation grew up under the image of their father as the sole driver behind the business. This behaviour reinforced the traditional patriarchal role within Asian families and the isolated nature of entrepreneurs. With this attitude it follows that the fathers would not acknowledge any support given to them, including by their wives. This then means that over time the founder ignores or chooses to forget the involvement of his wife within the business. This reinforces the findings of work by Ram and Holliday (1993), who argued that men, both in terms of financial rewards and recognition, exploited women in ethnic businesses. This attitude seemed to pass onto the next generation, who too did not identify any involvement of the mother within the business. These responses reinforce the notion that whilst the mother provides support backstage and this is crucial, it is not acknowledged. Furthermore this leads to the mother not to be considered an important player with the skills to aid negotiation of difficult transitions, such as succession between the two generations.

In these situations there was no particular event that had led to the withdrawal of the mother. Her involvement in the business had declined due to one of two reasons: either the business had outgrown her needs or the business had been consciously moved away from her and possibly other familial influence by the founder. The involvement of the mother in these cases followed a similar pattern, they had been very active in the business during the initial start-up phase but this had declined over time. The older respondents placed limited importance on her contribution to the development of the business.

One exception to this norm emerged in a particular case (B1), discussed earlier in this chapter. The mother had been actively involved in the business developing the marketing and owned this role until ill health had forced her complete withdrawal from the business:

> Early on she helped a lot. She wrote a recipe book and attended exhibitions. Now she has no active involvement in the business, but I discuss products and ideas with her. (Father)

> My mother was initially a very strong support to my father, but she has become very ill recently. When we were re-branding the product she went on road shows to exhibitions – such as The Ideal Home Show – and worked with an advertising agency to produce a cookbook as a way of introducing our ingredients and products. (Son)

The mother in this case was forced to retire from the business due to external circumstances. Both generations regarded her as an important force that had helped to build up the business and respected her involvement. In other cases the older generation had implicitly edged out the mother by reducing her importance within the business. Rather than being 'pushed' out of the business the mother in this case was ascribed significant status by active family members and could still influence business processes and decisions without having a formally active role. This in turn enabled the mother to act as a buffer between both generations. The significant difference between this case and those discussed earlier rests on the factors that instigated a decline in maternal involvement and the resulting perceptions of her involvement amongst both generations.

The mother as a buffer between both generations emerged as a concept where she helped to smooth the working relationships between the two generations. In order to be a buffer the mother had to have some involvement in the business that needed to be recognised by one or both generations. A buffer role within the family firm reinforces the hidden nature of maternal involvement during the transition dynamics, and is often a status unrecognised by either or both generational members. The complex nature of this position meant it was difficult to ask respondents directly whether the mother acted as buffer. Instead, the evidence for this was generated from answers relating to family dynamics. The most important question focused on whom each generation turned to when they had problems with the other family member. Indeed when describing the involvement of mothers they were usually relied upon to negotiate disputes between the two generations. The most common role in the buffer profile was for the mother to support the younger generation during disputes with the father or throughout periods of uncertainty:

> Initially my wife was a little worried, [my son] was very nervous about joining the business and taking on responsibilities. At first he would discuss things with my wife rather than directly with me, I didn't mind, but we try to be more open now. Although I know he still discusses things with my wife before coming to me.

Although the perceptions of buffer behaviour were generated through the interviews in an informal manner respondents were still able to control the degree of influence they ascribed to their partners. The older respondents, in particular those who acknowledged the involvement of their wives, maintained a clear limit on the degree of her importance within the business:

> She [wife] isn't actively involved in the business on a regular basis anymore, but our offices are based within our home, so she does get involved quite often.

> She doesn't get involved with the business too often, sometimes [my son] would discuss things with her and she would come to me, but that doesn't happen now.

These reactions represent the views across a range of the older respondents and highlight the importance of perception of maternal involvement by the older generation. Despite acknowledging her involvement the older generation needed to reinforce their omnipotence within the business. The findings and discussion in this paper highlight the sensitivities of this subject. Acknowledgement of the mother as a buffer within the business can undermine the founder's status ascribed by virtue of business success. As a means of reinforcing their own importance and control within a growing family business, founders may look to ways of minimising the impact of 'informal' labour sources from within the family. One such way founders attempt to do this is to move the business away from the influence of the family (and extended) members who are not actively involved in the business. Founders can use this as an opportunity to introduce new parameters within which they can negotiate a more professional relationship with the younger generation. This is only likely to occur where the founder aims to encourage a working relationship that does not replicate the father–child bond.

Whilst a professional relationship between father and son was nurtured through daily interactions, the mother maintained her behaviour by extending her maternal role within the family by maintaining harmonious relations. The above quote illustrates the dichotomy of the situation; as the two generations develop a professional relationship at work, at home the father still retains his paternal position. The mother is not present during their daily working interactions and so still perceives this relationship (father–successor) to reflect a parent–child bond. This scenario presents a double-edged issue for all family members. The mother is able to mediate the successor–heir relationship by her very role as a mother. This, however, reinforces the position of the successor as a child thereby reducing their attempts to present a professional front whilst simultaneously undermining the father's position of supremacy within the business.

This quote represents a case that had achieved this dual relationship between both generations. Other cases had worked towards this approach with varying degrees of success. In other cases the younger respondents had consciously reduced reliance on their mothers, one son described his father's reaction to the involvement of the mother:

> Yeah, he doesn't mind. It's more like a habit now. Now very rarely do I use my mum, at first it was a lot. The way me and my dad are now, we really can speak to each other about business matters. It's not like there's this barrier like there used to be. (Son)

> She has an influence. When [my son] wants something she talks to me, I usually give in. (Father)

> I don't talk to mum about the [business]. I speak to her about general matters but nothing to do with work ... She's very smart, she plays down the middle, not on either side. In front of me she supports my dad, and in front of my dad she's on my side. (Son)

For the son, as with other younger respondents the move away from relying on his mother represented a rite of passage. As the younger respondents became more confident of their position within the business and, more importantly, their relationship with the father they were willing to let go of the apron strings and assert their independence.

The mother as a buffer – A culturally specific phenomenon?

Relatively little work has focused on the role of mothers during succession, so it is impossible to make comparisons and determine whether this behaviour is specific to particular cultures. However, referring to the literature review it is possible to identify certain aspects of the Asian culture that may reinforce the importance of the mother's role within family firms. Work on entrepreneurship and family businesses continuously intersect with cultural perspectives and psychodynamic approaches. Whilst considerable research has focused on the importance of culture on ethnic entrepreneurship, ethnic aspects of family business research are a recently new area of research. However, the problems of applying existing models to family dynamics and business behaviour means the impact of cultural differences are often ignored. Most of the models applied to family business succession are based on empirical data drawn predominantly from Anglo-Saxon cases, which do not necessarily allow for differences amongst other ethnic groups. For example Bjerke's (1998) work on familial loyalty during business start-up and development amongst Malaysians was much greater compared to groups in the West. This reinforces the notion that the family is placed on an equal, if not higher, status than the individual.

The discussion earlier in this chapter concluded that filial obligation remains an important influence on the decision of the younger generation to join the family business and perform what they feel is their duty. Whilst some writers focus upon the generic parent–child relationship and the nature of obligation (Finch, 1989), others have developed this further introducing the influence of ethnic culture and tradition; for example, Ballard and Ballard (1984) present a discussion surrounding the concept of 'izzat'.[2] Writers argue this issue places significant stress upon the younger British Asian generation (Alibhai-Brown, 2000). The earlier discussion emphasised filial obligation as a significant factor in decision-making, which reinforces the notion that the younger generation places the family on a par, if not at a higher status, with their own needs. The very act of filial nature means that the younger generation is accepting to work within the patriarchal system of the business and the family and is less likely to rebel against existing power structures. As this discussion has shown, even where the father is keen to promote a more equal and professional working relationship the success of their relationship can still be attributed to the involvement of the mother working as a buffer.

As stated earlier it is difficult to understand whether this behaviour is applicable to all family firms regardless of ethnic background. At this point however, taking into account the lack of comparable research, one could argue the mother as a buffer is likely to be more apparent in Asian family firms because of the cultural factors that still influence the younger generation in Britain. Whilst this may change over time as successive generations alter their perceptions of cultural obligations, the role of the mother is still powerful and strengthened by her ambiguous role in the business.

Notes

1. The mother of the successor and also wife of the founder or outgoing family member.
2. Izzat wears honour and is used by these authors within the context of maintaining family pride by expected norms of behaviour among subsequent generations.

7
New Frontiers – The American South Asian Experience

Introduction

South Asian migration to the USA has lagged behind the settlement of the Diaspora to other countries. The relatively new population of first-generation South Asian migrants have a strong starting base than their counterparts had both in terms of internal (educational) resources and the opportunities in the wider economy. This chapter draws together various aspects of the debate on ethnic entrepreneurship in the United States to create a platform for the next chapter that will discuss the findings from the case studies in more detail. The first section begins with an overview of literature specific to the United States. The next section generates a profile of the South Asian community and, more specifically, the Indian and Pakistani groups (including the East African Asian community) based on the recent 2001 Census figures.

Ethnic entrepreneurship in the United States

The American cases are businesses that are less than twenty years old. Migrants who came from the Indian sub-continent over the last twenty years developed these businesses. Although economic and social conditions for the new entrants were far better compared to those faced by the previous generation in the 1960s and 1970s there is still a propensity for the first-generation migrants to enter self-employment as the primary career route. Figures on population and policy research estimate that 7.6 per cent of Asians from the Indian sub-continent own their own business (Noah, 1991).

Research focusing on ethnic entrepreneurship in America is not as prolific as the debate in the United Kingdom. The seminal pieces of work in this area date back thirty years (e.g. Light's (1972) work on ethnic entrepreneurs); although other research has developed over time it presents a somewhat fragmented view of ethnic entrepreneurship. This is largely due to the scale of the United States and wide range of experiences. Ethnic research has focused on the entrepreneurial experiences of a wide range of ethnic groups: Koreans, Chinese, Japanese Mexicans and African Americans (Light, 1984; Portes and Bach, 1985; Light and Bonacich, 1988; Kasarda, 1989; Bates, 1997). The breadth has been countered by the lack of depth applied on a consistent level to ethnic entrepreneurship. Ethnic groups in Britain are smaller in size and provide more cohesive groups from which detailed data can be generated. The field of ethnic entrepreneurship in Britain has focused on certain groups (possibly to the detriment of others) and this has enabled researchers to build up a more detailed analysis of economic activity amongst certain ethnic groups and even sub-groups. The British South Asian community has been the main beneficiary of a considerable amount of research (Aldrich *et al.*, 1981; Waldinger *et al.*, 1990; Srinivasan, 1992; Ram and Smallbone, 2001) whereas this group has received relatively less attention in the United States by comparison (Greene, 1997; Bates, 1999).

Initially it may seem that thinking on ethnic entrepreneurship in the United States is more under-developed than studies in Britain. This can be strongly counteracted by understanding that the impact of the country's scale and greater fragmentation of different ethnic communities has meant that it has been far more difficult to generate a comprehensive understanding of ethnic entrepreneurship. Over time in the United States, there has been an increasing acknowledgement of the heterogeneity amongst the ethnic community, not only in terms of ethnicity, but also, as importantly, in terms of class and education attainment (Ibrahim and Galt, 2003). Ethnic entrepreneurship in the United States is based on similar characteristics as activity in other countries, a combination of internal and external factors. The families have migrated at a time when they are further along their own life cycle; usually resulting in the second generation being much older and more influential in the earlier stages of the business start-up process. Furthermore, both generations were more likely to have higher educational levels also improving the range and sustainabilities of capital for business development. Externally, the United States is a mature enterprising economy, with the benefits of experience accumulated over the last thirty years. New generations of migrants who start-up business find themselves in an environment far more conducive to entrepreneurship and enterprising activity.

An underlying principle that recurs in migrant ethnic entrepreneurship is the notion of ethnic embedded networks, the culturalist approach
focuses on the resources and capital generated primarily through co-ethnic
networks. The benefits of these resources become critical when individuals identify clear discrepancies between their real and perceived value,
returning once again to the social marginality status. Within this approach
a critical factor lies in the influence of human and other forms of capital.
Cultural variables provide an important distinction between ethnic
communities regarding entrepreneurial activity. Co-ethnic networks enable
international trading to develop with lower transaction costs due to the
presence of trusted informal networks as well as exploitation of accumulated knowledge of different areas (Bjerke, 1998). Networks based on
pre-existing bonds of loyalty amongst co-ethnics are particularly efficient
because these conditions reduce 'transaction costs' thereby creating 'low
cost cultural transmission units' (Landa, 1998).

Another perspective on human capital is the 'Old Institutional
Explanation' whereby the relationship between and within institutions
are shaped by individuals in the institutions (Ibrahim and Galt, 2003).
The institutions then also exert their own influence on the individual.
This approach provides a means by which the distinct characteristics of
different ethnic groups can be understood through greater analysis of
their institutional arrangements. This work is clarified through the sizeable
and growing body of research on social capital of ethnic communities
and resources generated through embedded ethnic networks (Kloosterman
et al., 1999; Kloosterman, 2000).

The notion of what constitutes critical resources for ethnic entrepreneurship is as provocative in the United States as it is elsewhere across
the globe. In contrast to Ibrahim and Galt's (2003) 'cultural stance'
position, Bates (1999) argues the traits and variables that lead to entrepreneurship are not linked to one's ethnicity. He adopts a more
economical perspective and drawing on comparisons across different
ethnic groups in the United States he argues the specific nature of human
capital of individuals influences their propensity to enter self-employment:

> Asserting that Asian Americans have high self-employment rates
> because they are Asian implies that some sort of race specific cultural
> uniqueness gives them an advantage over members of other races.
> The fact that advanced education and wealth provide entry into
> self-employment has an altogether different implication... Asian
> Americans lacking human and financial capital do poorly when they
> pursue self-employment. Variations in self-employment outcomes

are consistently closely related to human and financial capital: people with an advanced education, work experience, and financial resources consistently do well in small businesses. (1999: 40)

In his assault on cultural influences on ethnic entrepreneurship Bates (1999) acknowledges how different generations respond to economic opportunities. This highlights how social capital develops over time in response to qualities of the groups. Research on ethnic embedded networks highlight limitations of networks generated amongst the first-generation ethnic migrants due to restricted integration both socially and economically (Kloosterman *et al.*, 1999). As successive generations achieve greater integration through processes of socialisation and education their range of resources is not solely limited to their ethnic group (Janjuha-Jivraj, 2003). The time lag between generations has a significant influence on self-employment levels of migrant communities (Butler, 1991; Levenstein, 1995). The basis of this argument inevitably lies in discrimination experienced by first-generation migrants resulting in blocked socio-economic mobility (Srinivasan, 1992). However this view provides a very simplistic approach to understanding ethnic entrepreneurship particularly when it transcends generations and remains a characteristic of certain ethnic communities – for example the Jewish community (Butler and Herring, 1991). Butler (1999) argues:

> Put another way, variations in self-employment among majority group members may still need the components of culture (and the history of exclusion and being in the 'stranger category') to help explain variation in the rate of self-employment. (1999: 188)

The example of the Jewish community is particularly applicable to the American Asian community. Both groups of migrants have strong familial and co-ethnic ties that generate the range of capitals required for entrepreneurship and, more importantly, business growth from initial start-up. Furthermore, in spite of high academic achievement both groups still maintain an entrepreneurial streak in the economy. This is likely to be a combination of facts resulting from the 'push–pull' classifications.

Asian business start-up – New frontiers

Asian entrepreneurship is on the cusp of new development in the United States of America. The profile of South Asian immigrants presents an interesting combination of individuals with limited skills and experiences to the large number of highly skilled migrants attracted to growing opportunities in the Silicon Valley (Kanjanapan, 1996; Saxenian, 2002). A high proportion of the South Asian population settled in the United States between 1990 and 2000; those in the Indian and Pakistani categories have the highest levels of education attainment amongst migrant ethnic communities. The time lag effect builds on the notion that successive generations increase their levels of education and thereby have access to greater resources surpassing the previous generations. The range of capital successive generations are able to draw upon is not limited to their co-ethnic community as there is greater socio-economic integration. The combination of recent migration along with high levels of education has created an interesting phenomenon amongst the Asian community. They have a significant capital base to draw resources from and this is likely to be extended beyond their own ethnic network.

The level of education inevitably affects the economic choices or opportunities available to migrants. As Saxenian (2002) states a significant level of highly qualified Asian migrants have flocked to Silicon Valley. Over time their activity has turned from employment to self-employment, leading to a breed of entrepreneurs known as The IndUS Entrepreneurs (TIE), described by Chabria (2000) as 'shepherds' guiding the next generation of start-ups. TIE estimates that 28,250 Indians were based in Silicon Valley in 1990, furthermore this ethnic group runs 67 per cent (774 out of 11,443) of the high-tech firms operating since 1980 (Saxenian, 1998). Numerous reports have focused on how this economic activity has erupted and gained momentum in an unexpected twist as many successful Indian entrepreneurs are re-locating by returning to India, an increasingly common practice nicknamed as B-to-B (back to Bangalore) or B-to-C (Back to Chennai) (Biers and Dhume, 2000; Ybarra, 2001).

Whilst high-tech enterprising activity has attracted most press and research attention there is another dimension to Asian entrepreneurship across other areas in the United States. In the other states, with large concentrations of the South Asian population, the traditional 'bricks and mortar' businesses have flourished. These businesses are not built on the basis of high academic qualifications instead they are rooted in social capital generated across migrating families and kinsfolk. These are individuals who are more likely to find themselves at odds with economic opportunities in the United States of America. Their skills may not match the needs of the economy or generate the income they require to sustain their family. These experiences may well provide these 'push' factors for entrepreneurship. This, however, is balanced by the considerable amount of social capital they are able to draw upon, creating a favourable environment to nurture entrepreneurship.

Ethnic entrepreneurship generated through social capital has been a critical factor in sustaining 'chain migration' (Ballard and Hurst, 1994). Through this system new migrants were able to find low-skilled employment opportunities in co-ethnic owned businesses. With the same copycat approach certain industries became popular, namely the retail sector: gas stations, motels fast food franchises and jewellery stores. Entrance into these businesses has been typically through the route of employment initially as a cashier, eventually leading to management promotions. For a large proportion of South Asians the leap from employee to entrepreneur occurred through co-ethnic support. Employees accumulated their experience in the organisations taking on more responsibilities eventually enabling them to take on senior management positions. The route to entrepreneurship from these positions was often through creating a partnership with their employers to open a new unit, sharing profits. Such links are reinforced by the experiences of migration (Werbner, 1981; Ward and Jenkins, 1984). This provided a sense of risk-reduction as new entrepreneurs were able to learn from the mistakes of fellow community members. The community was not settled enough to be in a position of competing with each other and this encouraged support through sharing of experiences and possibly even contacts. Drawing on examples from Britain, for many South Asian migrants low barriers to entry determined which industries were deemed as particularly attractive for business start-up. However, this also meant in certain industries over time there was an over-population of South Asians, particularly in the sectors such as retail (Rafiq, 1990; Deakins *et al.*, 1996) and hotels and catering (Curran and Burrows, 1988). These patterns have been replicated amongst the South Asian business community in the United States with a large concentration in the hotel and motel sector (Marger and Hoffman, 1992: 973).

The human capital that flourished through close ethnic ties created opportunities for rapid expansion of businesses in these sectors. Work by Kloosterman *et al.* (1999) on embedded ethnic networks identifies the diverse nature of resources that emerge from co-ethnic labour. These experiences of migration leading to group cohesion replicate Bourdieu's (1985) approach to social capital and in particular highlight the accrued benefits of cultural capital (cited in Portes, 1998). The resources generated from cultural capital focus explicitly on the ability to exploit resources through co-ethnic contacts. The experiences of this phase of Asian migrants reinforces this as the first generation of this community have access to cultural community, however this is largely limited to the parameters of the sub-group. For many of the more recent first generation, integration has been largely sporadic resulting in greater co-ethnic group solidarity (Portes, 1998). He goes on to argue that within bounded ethnic communities there is a critical factor influencing the development and allocation of resources, that is the altruistic nature of donors is finite. The cultural capital for this community has originated from their ability to exploit their entrepreneurial potential along with emphasis on education and willingness to provide a wide range of support to their kinsfolk.

The nature of social capital in this context and its impact on the generation of chain migrants once again draws attention to the notion of reciprocity and obligation. Support is offered to community members without expecting direct reciprocity. The nature of tight-knit communities requires individuals who have received help to find a way to pay that support forward to the next wave of families or individuals who require support in migration and settlement. Through membership of the co-ethnic community pressure is exerted on members to behave in accordance with socially acceptable norms, including providing support to subsequent community migrants. Portes (1998) argues the power of the community should not be underestimated in its influence on minimising deviant behaviour. The growth of ethnic enclaves associated with the migration of community members has further reinforced this behaviour:

> social capital is not contingent on direct knowledge of their benefactor, but on membership in the same group . . . In other words trust exists in this situation precisely because obligations are enforceable, not through recourse to law or violence but through the power of the community. (Portes, 1998: 28)

Ironically referring back to the experiences of South Asian entrepreneurs in Silicon Valley in spite of their education and range of professional experience those who have successfully ventured into their own business acknowledge their success to the initial start-up propelled by co-ethnic membership. Angel investors cited as the core of this group identify business opportunities both in their professional appointments as well as personal and social activities, including parties, religious festivals in Temples and restaurants (Clark, 2000). The same article quotes an individual who states membership of TIE is practically the only way in which South Asian entrepreneurs can realise their dreams. Although these experiences are anecdotal and do not carry the weight of empirical research they do suggest the need for further research in this area. Whilst work has been conducted amongst other ethnic groups across countries (Butler *et al.*, 2003) the impact of co-ethnic bonds and link to education levels both in the United States and the Indian sub-continent are ripe for research.

Development of capital through education

As migration patterns of the South Asian community have somewhat lagged behind their counterparts in the UK (Mattausch, 1998) and even Canada (Marger and Hoffman, 1992) members, there is a greater proportion of the population who are first-generation migrants and therefore able to benefit from the resources accrued through greater social cohesion of the migrant community. This presents a somewhat different situation for the Asian Diaspora in the United States compared to others in the United Kingdom or Kenya. The notion of community and even family (or kinship) alters over time and in response to cultural influences (Stewart, 2003). As the Asian community in the United Kingdom moves towards the third generation various researchers have predicted varying effects on the solidarity of migrant ethnic communities as successive generations achieve greater socio-economic integration. Education, a factor so highly prized within the Asian community regardless of where they settle (Ballard and Ballard, 1984; Le, 2001), presents a double-edged sword for communities keen to maintain their cultural traditions. For many first-generation migrants education was regarded as a means by which their children could penetrate the professional market and navigate their way around labour force discrimination. The emphasis on education became a prized asset within communities as aspirations for the younger generation were elevated:

> Education ambition is so great that it is considered rather shaming if a son is not able to achieve some kind of professional or technical qualification. (Ballard and Ballard, 1984: 42)

Education provided the route by which subsequent members of the community would achieve integration. It also indicated which segments of the community were more open to the influences of the Western culture (Luthra, 1997). However this notion of a group willing to 'embrace the *rationalist* culture of the West' (Luthra, 1997: 22; my emphasis) had its own problems; the community has had to contend with through successive generations. Many first-generation parents in the United Kingdom concentrated on the opportunities generated through self-employment, they also retained stringent expectations on the younger generation in terms of their behaviour towards the family and community through the bonds of culture and tradition tightened through the experience of migration. Thompson (1974) argued many parents were unprepared for the wider implications of education on their children to the extent that through their experience they would 'run the risk of adopting ambitions that conflict with the family's expectations of them' (1974: 247).

The situation is somewhat different for Asian migrants in the United States – the time lag of migration means social, economic and political conditions are very different than those experienced by the swell of migrants to the West in the early 1970s. Whilst the first generation of migrants may still not have the educational qualifications required to enable them to achieve professional status they are more aware of the implications of education and better prepared for the effects it has on the family and even community structure. Indeed the community has been heralded as a success for their ability to realise the 'American dream' through their emphasis on education (Le, 2001):

> As the so-called 'model-minority' we are frequently portrayed as a bright, shining example of hard work and patience whose examples other minority groups should follow. (Le, 2001)

Figures from the 2000 Census reinforce these views. A higher proportion of Asians (44%) were qualified to Bachelor's level or higher, this compared with 24 per cent of the total population (Reeves and Bennett, 2004). A breakdown of the Asian population identified Indians and Pakistanis with the highest representation of those holding Bachelor's degrees or more (Reeves and Bennett, 2004). Table 7.1 illustrates the breakdown across the various educational classifications.

The higher level of education attained by the South Asian population in the United States creates a stronger base for the generation of various resources. As these resources manifest themselves through the various forms of capital – human, social and even financial – they in turn create a stronger base upon which individuals can build enterprising activity.

As previously discussed, entrepreneurship amongst the South Asian community in the United Kingdom initially relied almost exclusively on co-ethnic support through credit rotation programmes, soft loans and employment opportunities. Whilst the latter of these practices, informal loans and support in employment, are still common practices

Table 7.1　Educational attainment of ethnic migrants in the USA (2000)

	Less than high school graduate	High school graduate	Some college or associate's degree	Bachelor's degree or higher
Chinese	23.0	13.2	15.8	48.1
Filipino	12.7	14.9	28.6	43.8
Asian Indian	13.3	10.3	12.5	**63.9**
Vietnamese	38.1	19.1	23.4	19.4
Korean	13.7	21.6	20.9	43.8
Japanese	8.9	22.2	27.1	41.9
Cambodian	53.3	18.8	18.6	9.2
Laotian	49.6	24.4	18.3	7.7
Pakistani	18.0	12.9	14.8	**54.3**
Thai	20.9	17.5	23.1	38.6
Other Asian	19.1	16.3	23.2	41.4

Source: Adapted from 2000 Census (Reeves and Bennett, 2004).

in the United States amongst the South Asian migrant community, wider changes in society and greater openness in the finance market opportunities for business development are far more prolific. This is exemplified by the range of South Asian-operated businesses. Although the community still dominates the retail and service sector the scale of business is generally larger. In the United Kingdom Asian retailers have traditionally dominated the CTN sector, in the United States retailing activity is far broader than grocery stores, with a large proportion in gas stations and associated fast food franchises.

Over the last twenty years South Asian migrants to the United States have benefited from a combination of development enterprise-based economic and social policies along with the benefits of learning from the experience of pioneering migrants to Europe and Canada and even the earlier settlers in the United States to create businesses that bypass the early stages of high-risk single-unit retail outlets. In turn they have been able to draw upon the more advanced forms of social capital amongst their co-ethnic communities and create businesses that are more stable and able to grow at a faster rate than their counterparts in the 1970s and 1980s in the United Kingdom.

Dynasties – Asian family businesses

Much of the research on family firms has been dominated by academics in the United States, with a growing body of work slowly emerging in other areas across the globe. As discussed in the previous chapters family business research has gradually adopted a more integrated approach to incorporate elements beyond the founder and the business, namely the family and even wider community. As the field of family business matures various critiques have emerged that highlight deficiencies in the body of research (Brockhaus, 2004; Sharma, 2004; Zahra and Sharma, 2004). A consistent theme that arises focuses on the lack of emphasis on cultural and ethnic factors in family firms (Enz *et al.*, 1990; Cramton, 1993; Owen and Rowe, 1995; Kay and Heck, 2004). Whilst some research has addressed the relationship between familial culture and organisational and management practices of family firms (Dyer, 1986, 1988; Astrachan, 1988; Daily and Dollinger, 1991) there is still plenty of scope for further exploration. In terms of research on ethnic family firms, research in this field broadly follows patterns of research on ethnic entrepreneurship in the United States. It is arguable that the United Kingdom has a stronger body of cohesive work on ethnic family firms compared to the work in the United States with researchers exploring both the dynamic of family members involved in the business along with issues of inter-generational succession (Ram and Holliday, 1993; Chan and Janjuha-Jivraj, 2000; Janjuha-Jivraj and Woods, 2001).

The lack of research on family firms in the United States is somewhat surprising when one considers the momentum of research in the field of family businesses and the population of ethnic family businesses. Whilst it is difficult to identify the numbers of South Asian-based family firms in the United States due to both the lack of data collection in this field and the challenges of identifying such businesses, data on entre-preneurial activity provides a good starting base. South Asian self-employment figures in the United States are only available since 1989 (Fairlie, 2004). Over this period rates of self-employment within this ethnic group are argued to have peaked in 1992 (12.9%) before dropping to 9.4 per cent in 2000. In 2003 the figure had risen again to 10.4 per cent (Fairlie, 2004). It is reasonable to assume a significant proportion of the businesses that have started up in this community are built on the social capital generated not only from family but also the wider religious and ethnic communities.

8
Experiences of South Asian American Family Firms

Introduction

Of all the cases explored in this book the businesses based in the United States were the youngest, due to the more recent migration patterns of the community. The cases from the States illustrate the challenges faced by family businesses during the earlier stages of business formation and development. Unlike the Kenyan and British businesses these cases had not yet experienced inter-generational transition, however their start-up processes have required the involvement of both generations. The discussion that unfolds will highlight conflicting expectations of whether respondents expect these businesses to develop and become dynasties.

The issues discussed in this chapter reflect areas that have been highlighted throughout this book. The American-based businesses offer a different perspective to the issue of succession in South Asian family firms, the American cases are less than ten years old and the younger generation (i.e. the second generation) had already completed their education. The first part of this chapter explores their motivations for joining the business particularly as in these cases there is an opportunity cost for remaining in the family firm. The next section considers the impact of other family members on the working dynamics within the business; to reinforce previous discussions the focus once again will be on the role of the heir's mother (who is also the wife of the founder). The penultimate section will analyse broader working dynamics of family members and how this impacts the management style of the business. The final section will explore planning activities in these businesses and how both generations express their desires for the longer-term development of the business.

Business start-up

Profiles in the previous chapter illustrate higher than average levels of degrees and postgraduate degrees amongst the American South Asian community, however for many of the first-generation migrants entry into business was a combination of both push and pull factors. The cases in this study show that motivations for business start-up arise from a combination of insufficient opportunities for progression in employment combined with a desire for self-employment and the benefits associated with entrepreneurship along with the ability to utilise embedded ethnic networks (Kloosterman *et al.*, 1999). Family members working in a range of low-skilled manual jobs preceded entrepreneurial opportunities. Often employment was offered through co-ethnic networks that had already established businesses. Initially the jobs available were primarily serving customers in retail outlets such as jewellery stores, gas stations, fast food franchises and motels. These jobs suited the new arrivals who had limited exposure to the American business environment.

Over time the employees built up experience and were able to take on increased responsibilities culminating in senior managerial roles; this created new opportunities for both sides as the newly promoted employees offered a route to business expansion for the employers. As many of these businesses were retail-based they had the typical characteristics associated with such firms: long operating hours, handling large amounts of cash and management of a team of staff as well as close contact with customers. These businesses benefited from the involvement of tight-knit families or kinships who share values of loyalty, hard work, deferred gratification and of course trustworthiness (Ram and Holliday, 1993). In these cases the employees were not related to their employers and although they were members of the same ethnic and even religious community the emotional distance between the individuals was sufficient to create a need for an additional source of motivation for commitment to the business; this was achieved by employers creating entrepreneurial opportunities through expansion. Employers entered into partnership agreements with co-ethnic managers who had performed well and generated sufficient trust and credibility, these managers invested a set amount for the purchase of a new retail outlet for a gas station or fast food franchise along with the commitment to run the business. As time progressed they then had the option to buy out their former employers. This was the means by which a number of respondents were able to achieve the transition from employee to employer. In addition to the financial opportunities, these partnerships enabled social capital to develop and flourish reinforcing the notion of chain support for successive migrants and their families.

Entrepreneurship amongst this group was a combination of push and pull factors, however in some of the cases highlighted there was no option but to go into business. They had come to the United States driven by a desire to create their fortune through enterprise and hard work and an unflinching resolve to go into business. Such was the determination to initiate this dream that in extreme cases they bypassed the steady progressive approach described above and invested all their time and energy in identifying business opportunities. In one such case the father and his brother moved from New York to Kansas in a bid to find business opportunities. They networked themselves into the business community whilst gathering information on viable opportunities whilst the wife of one worked as a chambermaid and supported the family. After two months they received a phone call from a gas supplier who offered them a run-down gas station that was on the market. These illustrations represent the 'pull' factors, the motivations and access to resources that are identified by researchers as the more positive associations of entrepreneurship – cultural traits (Ram and Jones, 1998) and forms of support through embedded co-ethnic capital (Kloosterman *et al.*, 1999). However there were the push factors leading to self-employment – experiences of discrimination and 'blocked social mobility'.

The only female founder of a business amongst the American cases (A3a, Appendix 3) had previously been working in the corporate sector as a secretary. She had graduated from university with a Degree in Business Administration and had a number of professional and IT-based courses. She and her husband had set up a confectionery shop. As both husband and wife built up their experience and confidence in running a business they began to consider other retail-based businesses. During this time the mother started to experience difficulties in her working relationship with a new boss:

> I started to work under a new manager who undermined me and what I could do. He kept questioning my capabilities and my work and so I left. It was harassment, discrimination. I had been involved with businesses before, and I decided to keep going in business instead.

The next business, a delicatessen, was set up with the mother at the helm rather than her husband, as this was her project. As the 'co-preneurial' (Marshack, 1994) team became more involved in the operations of that business their daughter took over the confectionery store, which was later sold after her marriage. The deli was built up to a successful business and then sold, this then enabled the family to move into the gas station sector.

In another cases the experience of the first generation echoed the frustrations of blocked opportunities, although the stimuli for moving into self-employment was far less traumatic than it had been in the earlier case. In another example the father (A2a, Appendix 3) had been working in the retail banking sector since his migration to the United States in 1982. He had a degree in Commerce from Pakistan and also received industry-based training whilst working in the States. He had been in the position of bank teller for five years before being promoted to Vice President. At this point he realised he had reached his limit as promotional prospects past vice-presidency were highly unlikely. This realisation, along with pressure from his father to go into business, encouraged him to consider entrepreneurial ventures.

The experiences of his entry into business were less clearly defined as either push or pull factors. The encouragement of his father created a more favourable response to entrepreneurship and this was further enhanced by the broader range of resources available through his family, namely other brothers who were also committed to supporting a business. The respondent and his wife bought a convenience store in partnership with his two brothers in California. Initially all three brothers continued their jobs. However the husband and wife eventually brought themselves out to start a business on their own. A2a resigned from the bank and bought a liquor store. From this base he increased the number of retail units before moving to Texas and generating new business.

Business start-up described in these cases once again reinforces the impact of family ties both as a resource and stimuli for entrepreneurial activity. Whilst the two cases varied in the resources they had available for business development they both shared similar traits of utilising whatever they had available in the initial stages of business development. In the latter case A2a's motivation for business start was further fuelled by his desire to support his brothers and comply with his father's advice. This initial desire to provide for the wider family was as strong to motivate business development as the negative experiences of A3a in wanting to leave her working environment of discrimination.

Aspirations of the younger generation

The entry of the younger generation into the businesses was not a result of life-long expectations from either generation. Motivations to start-up the businesses were primarily based on respondents looking for a means by which they could support themselves and their families. Therefore the businesses had not been developed with the aim of becoming dynasties nor were there plans to incorporate the younger family members into the business. Entry of the younger generation into the business happened incrementally and also as a result of opportunities through business growth. None of the younger generation had been 'formally' groomed to join the business however they had experienced working in the business from a young age and this provided the subtle, but important, factors influencing their decisions to join the business.

The younger generation from the American cases were all educated to degree level, in some cases having graduated with two Bachelor's degrees. They had grown up with the expectation that they would enter professions and achieve the transition towards professions that had evaded their parents. Whilst growing up and completing their education the younger respondents had also been called upon to help out in the business. Previous discussions in this book have emphasised the importance of informal familial support as a critical factor in the success of business development. The involvement of children in family businesses as unpaid labour during holidays and out of school provides one of the most important forms of support for such businesses (Song, 1999). These experiences of younger members in family business invariably generate mixed emotions of pride and resentment. The nature of the experience will undoubtedly have an impact on the way the younger generation view their involvement in the business, however the factors that influence this are strongly based on how the younger generation felt external stakeholders (i.e. customers, clients and peers) reacted to the business (Chan and Janjuha-Jivraj, 2000). This research compared the experiences of British South Asian and Chinese second generations who had been involved in the family businesses. Where the younger generation worked in businesses that were heavily embedded in a typical ethnic market they were more likely to face racism and were more hostile to the idea of continued involvement in the business. This was prevalent amongst the Chinese respondents most of whom came from businesses in the Chinese catering sector. The South Asian respondents by contrast came from a much broader range of businesses that had greater integration with other non-ethnic businesses, ranging from hotel and catering to retailing. They had not suffered the experience of racism associated with the businesses. In these cases the South Asian respondents had similar levels of education to the Chinese respondents but were more open to the idea of working in the family business in the future.

The motivations for the younger generation from the American cases in joining the business all followed the same pattern; they had considered or even started working in the professional field but the lure of the family business was a far more attractive proposition. Often this interest had been ignited by their involvement in the business from a younger age that had steadily increased as they became older and more confident.

> To begin with I wanted to go into Engineering but as I became more interested in business I shifted my studies towards Commerce and I developed a passion for Economics . . . I had researched Engineering as a career but I only had a small interest in becoming a professional, to me employment had limited progression, climbing the ladder would be a step by step process. In business you can skip steps based on your performance.

> I worked hard for 'IBM' [in California] but it was always the same paycheck and this was not enough to motivate me. Whether I worked hard or less I was paid the same amount. I wanted to work hard and feel like I had really reaped the benefits of my effort. I had always been involved in the business and so I moved to Dallas and tried working with my Dad to get a feel for the business.

For the younger generation their exposure to the business had created positive feelings towards business involvement and working with the family. Their ability to choose the business over a career was also an important factor in reinforcing their commitment towards entrepreneurship. Where they had been exposed to the business at a younger age they reflected their experiences had been positive:

> I worked with 'AT and T' for a year as an engineer, the money was good but I wasn't really interested in following it as a career. I was more interested in being my own boss. I had been involved in the businesses we had in Pakistan and here in the States, initially my job had been to man the cash register. I really enjoyed working in the business, I got to learn about finances and marketing at a young age.

My dad had wanted me to get involved with the business, he was busy with the business and needed me. He paid me when I was fifteen, four dollars fifty an hour...My thinking is in tune with the business, I never seriously considered working elsewhere. I did spend two months working as a sales persons in a cell phone retail outlet but this was to get exposure into a new business.

Exposure to the business during childhood created a greater sense of confidence and willingness to take risks in addition to nurturing the other traits associated with entrepreneurial behaviour (Stanworth and Gray, 1991). The manner by which South Asian entrepreneurs expanded their businesses through diversification created better opportunities for the younger generation to test their enterprising skills in a somewhat controlled manner. Perhaps in response to more flexible market with greater opportunities, the route of business expansion for many South Asian-based entrepreneurs has been through diversification. Their entrepreneurs have created portfolios of businesses across different sectors, however they build upon their experience and economies of scale by working in the retail sector and creating strategic alliances through the use of franchises wherever possible. By building up a track record either with gas suppliers or with franchisers the older generation were able to create a springboard for the younger generation to develop their own businesses by setting up retail units they managed. The younger generation had the experience of working with their parents, they had established some credibility with potential partners and also had the support of family members as guarantors. This enabled them to consider working on different projects on their own or even with other family members thereby adding to the portfolio of family-based business activities. In one case for example, the son worked with his father in running a chain of nine gas stations across Dallas and Kansas, he had also set up businesses with other family members; a seasonal Christmas gift shop with his sister on a short-term lease as well as another general gift shop with his fiancé. The family's strategic direction for the business was to move towards more large-scale projects. Their expansion had been previously based on buying run-down gas station sites that they renovated and then managed. They had now turned their attention to buying new locations that would enable them to build gas stations and retail outlets from scratch and therefore allow them to invest in larger projects with better returns. In order to achieve this shift in business operations the son had moved from managing stores to overseeing the construction of two projects they were working on in Kansas. The growth of these businesses and range of activity in the family's portfolios emphasise the flexible approach to entrepreneurship. This approach to running business meant both generations have been able to focus on the growth aspects of entrepreneurship.

Family members

The businesses started up with a combination of resources drawn from family members. The range of support varied from financial investment and providing manpower during the initial stages of start-up to motivation and morale boosting and emotional support. As the businesses developed the composition of family members involved changed to reflect the different needs. The most common pattern that emerged was the involvement of the wives of the founders during the start-up period of the business and then their eventual withdrawal. The businesses were the result of combined effort of the husband and wife team, acting as 'copreneurs' (Marshack, 1994). The initial stages of the business were based on the 'copreneurial' team working together in running all aspects of the business. In one case the wife took on the role of breadwinner, working as a chambermaid to support the family whilst her husband and brother-in-law explored various business opportunities. Although these cases had wider family members who provided the stability or forms of support for business start-up the nature of the businesses required trusted manpower and the wives were recruited to help organise the businesses. Their role in these businesses reinforced the profile of women in family firms identified by Ram and Holliday (1993) and Dhaliwal (1998) emphasising the exploitative nature of female involvement in such organisations. The mothers represented a critical factor in the success of the business during the start-up period but as the business developed and absorbed the resources of other family members and individuals the contribution of the mother diminished, she was regarded by active family members as no longer necessary to the business:

> Initially my mother was involved in the business when it was starting. She was involved until 1995 or 1996 but once it settled and we had a stable income there was no need for her to work. She was able to spend more time with the family. Now it's not viable for her to be involved in the business. (Son)

My wife is not involved in the business anymore. Previously she was needed to help when we were starting up, but not anymore. (Father)

In another case the wife had been very active during the initial start-up phase of the business, particularly when her husband had sold the business to his brothers and relocated in a bid to start up a business independently of his family. Over time the son and his wife had become involved in the business and the mother's role became far more involved with the daily activities of running the business. The son described how his mother's influence in the business shifted as her vision for the business no longer matched the strategic direction of the organisation:

My mum is not business-minded. She has a different perspective. My dad takes a broad perspective, he thinks big but my mum has a small business mentality. For example Dad will spend fifty thousand dollars on advertising, Mum wouldn't. I'm somewhere in between.

All four family members were involved in decisions regarding the business; discussions regarding the business usually occurred informally during dinner time. The son considered his mother and wife had some influence, albeit limited, in business decisions, his father on the other hand did not refer to his wife's involvement at all. The attitude of the older generation has similarities with some of the British cases where the older respondents exerted a strong patriarchal culture in both their businesses and families.

Another case (A3) presented a very different scenario, the husband and wife became copreneurs to start up a business, however instead of decreasing her involvement in the business the wife not only remained actively involved but became the stronger partner as the business grew. Her husband remained the manager of one unit whilst she built up other retail units that were sold in order to buy bigger businesses. As the businesses grew both the children (a daughter and a son) became involved in the business, the daughter remained in the business until her marriage. The business has grown from a confectionery shop to three gas stations. Areas of responsibility were split with the wife controlling financial decisions whilst her husband was responsible for the daily management of the units along with the son who divided his time between the family business and his own project, a mortgage company.

None of the cases had daughters involved in the business as a long-term commitment. Where they had been operating units or supporting the business this was a short-term measure and usually terminated once they were married. This reflects the cultural norms of the families whereby daughters were no longer considered part of the family following their marriage. This does however provide an interesting contrast to the Kenyan examples where the third generation did include daughters who were running the businesses alongside their brothers. Over time the American cases may face similar options as the pool of potential heirs diminishes.

Dynamics of generations working in the family firm

The relationships between the two generations in the American cases operated in a culture that was very patriarchal. The fathers had strong personalities that dictated both family and business culture. Although the older family members had not expected their children to join the business they were determined the younger generation members would help in the business as they were growing up. This in turn led to the younger generation remaining in the business on the completion of their studies. This occurred as a natural progression rather than as the result of explicit grooming or sudden shock events requiring their entry. Both generations described their working relationships as good, they acknowledged disagreements they faced over business decisions but also talked about how they managed to resolve the problems. Often this entailed both generations discussing the issue and finding a solution, in extreme cases where things became very emotional they would calm down before tackling the situation. Where it was not always easy to find a mutually acceptable solution the father still seemed to pull rank and override the final decision.

The relationships between the two generations seemed to be strengthened by a number of factors, the younger generation having worked in the business from a young age had a great deal of exposure to the mechanics of the business as well as the way in which the family operated. In addition although the father was very domineering, the younger generation had managed to create their own working space by setting up separate businesses in addition to the main family firm. This also helped the younger generation assert themselves in the family firm both with family and non-family staff. An additional benefit of this has also meant the older generation was more willing to engage in discussions concerning the longer-term plans for the business with the younger generation. In one case where plans were starting to take shape the older respondent was gradually withdrawing from the business:

> My relationship with [my son] is very good, we have an open relationship. I use my instinct a lot in business and he generally listens. About 99.9 per cent of the time he will listen, but he does make his own decisions at times. I am gradually moving out of the business, we have commitments overseas I am focusing on. In the meantime he is taking over, in a few months he will completely take over the businesses here ... I don't plan to retire yet, maybe in the next four or five years but I'm not working in the business everyday.

The responses of his son, echoed these views and stressed how the father and son relationship had improved considerably since they had started working together:

> Our relationship is much better now. Previously we didn't spend time together. There was no communication. Now we have learnt to respect each other more, you don't get respect unless you get it. My mum is also happier now we communicate more, we are better as a family, we are more cohesive and work together well. My plan is to keep running the business for the next four years, after that then maybe sell it and invest in something else or maintain it and start something else. My Dad will retire, but this is his responsibility, everyone is responsible for their own retirement. He needs to be responsible to save money for himself.

There were similar attitudes in another case as the father had prepared to take a back seat in the business. He had already sold his shares in the business to his son for a nominal amount, his son now had the control to move the business into different directions and exploit new business opportunities. The son also highlighted an additional benefit of the positive working relationship with his father; their personal relationship had improved a great enabling them to become far closer:

> It's closer now because I share personal problems with him. Previously I used to discuss things with my sisters now I talk to my Dad. He understands me and I suppose he lets me have my way more than he does with other family members. I think he has more respect for me now. My mum isn't aware of our relationship and how close we are. My mum thinks she is the most important person for the family.

Dad and I are close, but she is naïve about this, she doesn't know when we talk about personal things.

In the third case the relationship between the parents and the son had been described as always good and open, although the mother did acknowledge she had mediated the relationship between her husband and son. The son was very positive about his relationship with his parents but did acknowledge the difference between the two of them:

Work is work, I don't work hand in hand with Dad. We have separate working routines and this hasn't affected our relationship. It's amazing we have a good relationship, best friends. I understand Mum a lot more, she has become more dependent on me. I understand their financial position more and I can support them more. They had initially planned their retirement, but it didn't work. I'm their retirement plan.

The relationships in these cases do not fall into antagonistic patterns previously described in the literature on working dynamics of family members (Kets de Vries, 1996). However the critical difference in these businesses compared to other family firms lies in the position of the younger generation. They are not completely dependent on the family business as they have interests in external investments. In addition they are more likely to gain greater acceptance and credibility for their enterprising activities on the success of their own businesses both by family members and other individuals involved in the family firm. They have been able to navigate one of the most difficult aspects of being an heir – proving their worth by engaging in other business activities. This in turn means their fathers are more willing to relax control over the business and think about preparations for inter-generational transition.

The above quotes highlight that as the working relationship improved, so too did the personal relationship. It is interesting in two of these cases the mothers were not recognised as being buffers between the generations, this may be because the dynamics between the fathers and sons did not require this intervention, or because they chose not to acknowledge the role of the mother other than during the initial start-up phase. Where the mother was an active partner in the business, she had also had the opportunity to nurture the relationship between the generations both at home and at work.

In terms of business development both generations seemed to be quite synchronised with regards to their longer-term visions for both the business and the involvement of family members. This is one of the better indicators of how harmonious working relationships are between the generations, as it clearly indicates both generations have addressed or are at least starting to address the taboo subject of transfer of owner-ship and control, this in turn indicates greater stability for the business.

The American cases illustrate the new brand of South Asian family firms. These cases represent a significant transition from previous generations of family firms across the Diaspora. Migrants were able to start-up businesses, shifting their reliance onto the intellectual forms of human capital rather than emphasising the labour capital. The improved educa-tion status raised the level of quality and also effectiveness of support enabling entrepreneurs to fulfil higher aspirations for growth and portfolio entrepreneurship. The working dynamics between the two generations showed a clear distinction drawn from the patriarchal relationship dominant in their personal relationships. However, this was offset by the younger generation spreading their investments and risk. They were not completely dependent on the family business and this created a more equal and healthier relationship between parents and offspring.

9
Conclusions

Introduction

This chapter draws together key findings and trends of businesses across the three countries. The issues discussed in this chapter highlight how family businesses in different areas of the Asian Diaspora respond to challenges of inter-generational succession. The range of differences in terms of migration and settlement across the countries illustrate how members of the community integrate over generations and the impact this has on business and family dynamics. The field of family business research has increasingly acknowledged the importance of family – immediate, extended and wider kinship networks in the survival and development of businesses. This has been emphasised by the increasing activity on research in the field of social capital and ethnic embedded networks (Kloosterman *et al.*, 1999; Janjuha-Jivraj, 2004a).

The discussions in this book have emphasised how families and co-ethnic community members not only provide critical support for the initial start-up phase of the business through financial, labour, intellectual and emotional support but also continue to be integral to the development of the business. The central thrust to this book lies in how family members perceive their involvement and their behaviour vis-à-vis the business and family. Most of the work in the field of family businesses has been dominated by research on firms that are not Asian, and for a long time has not adopted an integrated approach between the family and the business. Researchers increasingly recognise gaps in the field of family business research, highlighting the largely homogenous profile of business, neglecting migrant ethnic communities that represent diverse cultural backgrounds as well as the role of women in such businesses. The cultural background of the family is a critical factor in the way family businesses operate, this has been acknowledged as research increasingly identify the link between familial culture and family businesses (Fournier an Lightfoot, 1996). Asian families provide a contrast in their cultural behaviour and norms compared to Anglo-Saxon families, although this is slowly changing with the gradual integration of successive generations; the differences in attitudes towards the family and individual provide a sufficient distinction to warrant work such as this to focus exclusively on the activities and behaviour of family businesses experiencing inter-generational transition. Bjerke's work on Chinese families and entrepreneurship presents a clear distinction (1998) of the different cultural backgrounds of families and the implications for family firms from an Asian background:

> In other words, the dichotomy individual society is not very applicable to the Chinese world. And the self-reliant individual, who single-handedly creates a new business venture against the common-sense beliefs all around him – or herself, is definitely not an adequate typification in the Chinese society. The smallest unit in society is rather the family. (Bjerke, 1998)

The impact of the family and wider co-ethnic kin ties who are also regarded as important as family (Wong, 1995) cannot be underestimated in the field of family business research. This approach has presented the underlying theme to the issues discussed throughout this book. The discussion in this chapter draws together the main issues affecting the cases experiencing inter-generational transition – namely the factors surrounding younger generation entry into the business, impact of social capital on the development of the business and involvement of the family, the impact of non-active family members, primarily wives of founders (mothers of heirs), and finally the working relationships of active family members.

Younger generation entry – Filial obligation

The events surrounding business entry were important influences on the resulting working relationship between the generations. Filial entry was split between businesses which were the result of long-term plans and familial expectation for younger generation entry – 'anticipated entry' – and surprise events such as lack of manpower, family ill-health or rapid business growth which propelled the entry of the younger generation into the business, often away from their own career or professions – 'unanticipated triggers'. Filial obligation is the most common form of obligation leading to younger generation business entry, however there are cases where the parents face considerable pressure from their children who want to join against the parents' wishes. This form of obligation, categorised as parental obligation generates a very different working environment and dynamic between the generations as they grapple with the emotions that arise from this method of business entry.

Business entry as a result of family expectations during the growth and development of the younger generation often resulted in top-heavy relationships between the father and the son. This reinforced the 'strong-father, weak-son relationships' identified by previous research (Levinson, 1971; Kets de Vries, 1996). This is generally expected, the younger generation had fulfilled parental expectations by joining the family business (in certain cases sacrificing their personal desires) and reinforced the father's position as head decision-maker both within the family and the business. Furthermore, as previously discussed, by joining the family business members of the younger generation were consciously accepting the authority structures within the family that were often reinforced within the business. This acceptance represented a high level of compliance within the parameters of the business, which often was an extension of the founder's personal value system.

The unanticipated obligatory triggers led to quite different dynamics between both generations. The nature of events surrounding unantici-pated obligatory triggers meant the older generation unexpectedly required the support of the younger generation in order to keep the business running. In these instances the survival of the business was crucial for the stability of the family and in certain cases this also included the extended family. In these cases, there were examples of the younger generation who had to leave their chosen profession or business in order to provide support to the family business. Within these cases the relationship between both generations was more balanced. In these cases the older generation had encouraged their children to develop their own careers, however circumstances meant that the younger respondents made a decision to support the business for the greater good of the family.

The older respondents were willing to acknowledge the actions of the younger generation and displayed gratitude towards their children. In these cases the younger generation had established their credibility in organisations external to the family business and this perhaps provided an additional means by which the older respondents were willing to delegate greater authority to their heirs. Although some of the cases under 'anticipated filial obligation' also had the younger generation developing external careers, this was largely undermined by the authority of the father. Within the unanticipated obligatory working relationships the more equal relationship enabled the younger generation to gain greater credibility within the business and with colleagues far quicker as the founder was working to enhance the position of his (or her) heir rather than undermine their authority. Another important factor influencing the founders' attitudes to encouraging a harmonious working relationship was explained by the realisation of their limitations within the business. The entry of the younger generation forced them to acknowledge they needed additional support in order to keep the business going. These were the only cases where the older generation exhibited vulnerability in their involvement with the business and the family.

These positive working arrangements, however, generated their own set of problems, particularly in the reactions from other family members both involved and external to the business. As both generations actively involved in the business moved towards a more professional working relationship, the integrated nature of the family and business amongst these cases meant that working relationship often spilled over into their domestic lives. For family members who had some distance from the business it was difficult to accept the even relationship between both generations in the domestic sphere, which maintained traditional values and cultural traits. This meant the younger respondents were caught between working with their father (or mother) as an equal at work and being forced back into the parent–child relationship at home.

In between these two extreme forms of business entry the American cases indicated the impact of the younger generation 'drifting' into the business having been exposed to it from a young age. Whilst the older generation did not explicitly state that they intended the younger generation to join the business in their quest to generate a family business, they did expect their family members to pitch in and support the development of the business. Although the younger respondents had achieved university degrees their own longer-term plans had been to work in the business, in their minds this was implied as the business needed their manpower. For these respondents there was no conflict, they had not developed professional trajectories however they were very keen on engaging in the entrepreneurial behaviour. Their involvement in the family business provided them with opportunities to develop their own businesses, often using familial resources and experience. This in turn created a more equal working relationship between the two generations as the younger generation did not have to work as hard to prove their worth to their father, other family members and even non-family staff. The success of their own businesses provided a testament to their business capabilities.

The other form of obligation that emerged in this research was 'parental obligation' which has been largely neglected in existing family business research. This area explored the impact on working relationships when the younger generation 'forced' their way into the family business. Initial thoughts on this approach expected the younger generation to fit the 'silver spoon' profile of family business entrants, described as taking the easy option. Paradoxically the younger respondents in these cases experienced the greatest difficulty establishing themselves within the business. In these cases the entry of the younger generation had a profound effect on their working relationship with the older respondents. The older generation had been forced into a position where emotional bonds meant they had to take on the younger generation, in some cases this meant not only restructuring the business but also adapting their future personal plans to incorporate the involvement of the younger generation. In these cases the older generation displayed resentment in the way their children had entered the business and this underpinned the resulting working relationship that ensued. Within these cases the working relationship was also top-heavy but the younger generation showed a determination to prove their worth unlike their contemporaries in the 'filial anticipated obligation' cases. This desire to show their worth was not only limited to the older generation but also extended to other stakeholders within the business (non-family employees, colleagues, customers) as well as other family members with varying degrees of involvement in the business. As a result the younger respondents were often reluctant to display their weaknesses to the older generation and therefore sought alternative sources of support within the business rather than approaching their fathers for help. Over a longer period the younger generation still felt they had not been able to achieve complete acceptance for their decision to leave education and join the business despite their considerable success in exploiting new and very successful opportunities.

When business entry obligation was identified as a research focus for this thesis it was expected that there would be a significant number of younger respondents who fulfilled their filial responsibilities by joining the business as expected by family members. Work on preparing for family business succession identifies the importance of identifying an heir and gaining their consent to joining the business (Kuratko, 1995). However this research has shown that such approaches merely serve to reinforce the founder's approach to running the business as the working relationship between the generations remains very top-heavy with little or no opportunity for the younger generation to assert their authority within the business. Butler-Cole (1975) argues the founders will endeavour to ensure the successors emulate their views and business style thus reinforcing their presence within the business. The weakness of this approach to the resulting working relationship was evident in the conflicting long-term views of both generations. This was made even more difficult as both generations were making plans independently of each other, potentially leading to serious conflicts for the long-term survival of the business. Ironically the approach least favoured by successional models, the unexpected emergence of an heir, facilitated the most harmonious and productive working relationship between the generations. This can be explained by factors such as the founders' gratitude to the younger generation for stepping in and the realisation of their own limitations within the business.

Reliance on family and co-ethnic resources

Discussions throughout the book explored how successive generations in different countries adapted their involvement and reliance on family and co-ethnic support. The central thrust in this section explored how the social capital of family and community provided critical support during the process of business start-up and development through the evolution of embedded ethnic networks. The literature underpinning this research area originated from the extensive work on social capital of ethnic migrants (Portes, 1998; Kloosterman *et al.*, 1999; Marger, 2001; Adler and Kwon, 2002). Sanders and Nee (1987) highlight the inevitable decline of reliance on informal ethnic solidarity as successive generations become further integrated with the mainstream and reduce their reliance on ethnic resources to fulfil their needs. Considerable work on ethnic entrepreneurship highlighted the social capital of ethnic entrepreneurs as a critical resource in the start-up and development of their business, classified by Ram and Jones (1998) as falling under the 'culturalist tradition' (Ward and Jenkins, 1984; Srinivasan, 1992; Curran *et al.*, 1993; Basu, 1995). In exploring the attitudes across both generations of the emphasis on ethnic resources for business development, this research assessed the centrality of these resources to business development and the viability of the 'culturalist tradition' in explaining the success of the Asian businesses in this research.

Attitudes towards co-ethnic support generated widely differing reactions from the two generations. As expected most of the older generation displayed strong emotional and loyal bonds to their ethnic networks. This originated from various factors, either they had drawn upon specific resources during the start-up or development of their business or the wider support from the community had provided an important buffer for their settlement during their migration. In certain cases this sense of loyalty was very evident in the way respondents described their relationship with their religious-ethnic community; whilst they had negative experiences with members or felt the nature of support had changed significantly over time they were careful to mini-mise their criticisms. For other older respondents their approach to the ethnic community was more unexpected as they consciously chose to distance their business success from any involvement with the community. In the analysis these respondents were identified as indi-viduals who demonstrated a very strong internal locus of control and through the discussion of the previous research questions were individ-uals who could be described as strongly patriarchal both at home and in the business.

The most interesting cases in this section were the businesses that had benefited from community resources through networks and access to additional resources through business expansion (as was later revealed through other cases who were partners), however both generations in the business denied any involvement with the community. The views from the older respondents represented a range of responses illustrating their different stages of development in terms of sustained reliance on the ethnic community and integration with the mainstream community. As discussed earlier some of the respondents acknowledged a change in their relationship with the ethnic networks that had resulted in a decline in their involvement and reliance on these resources, however they still maintained a strong emotional bond towards the community. The latter cases in this paragraph illustrated respondents who clearly differentiated themselves from the community, both in terms of business as well as socially and even religiously. The integration of older generation through achieving business success and securing a stable foundation for future family members meant that the ethnic solidarity of both the wider South Asian community and religious-ethnic sub-groups reduced in terms of business emphasis. There was a prevailing attitude amongst most of the older respondents who felt that the religious-ethnic community still represented a focal point for their religious and social needs.

The younger respondents showed a more critical and objective approach when assessing their relationship with the co-ethnic community. The younger generation varied in the nature and depth of their relationships with the community. Factors highlighted by Sanders and Nee (1987), such as education and degree of professional and social integration, were felt to have an impact on reduced emphasis on the ethnic networks and these were identified as influencing the nature of the relationship for the younger respondents. Attainment of a university degree represented a significant distinction in the attitudes of the younger generation towards ethnic involvement. The experiences of socialisation with wider ethnic groups and the resulting confidence meant the younger genera-tion could seek resources beyond their ethnic resources. Very few younger respondents described any sort of business involvement with their ethnic community, however a wider number felt they were actively involved with the community for their social and religious needs as well as providing a foundation for their identity.

The overall behaviour that emerged from responses of the younger generation was their greater objectivity and conscious distance from the community. Many of the younger respondents had a clear definition of the relationship with their ethnic network unlike the mixed views sometimes expressed by the older respondents. Although the younger generation did not consider relying on the ethnic community for business-based resources – in fact many respondents had been very proactive in generating contacts with other formal business organisations – they still turned to the community to fulfil other needs. This suggests that rather than a natural decline of community activity amongst subsequent generations, as predicted by researchers such as Modood (1992), the younger generation is changing the nature of its relationship with the co-ethnic community rather than withdrawing completely.

The changing nature of the resource-based relationships amongst the younger respondents illustrated how the younger generation were attempting to move the business away from relying on the community towards a more professional approach in terms of the resources utilised within the business. This involved the younger generation drawing upon resources based on the experiences and qualifications of service providers rather than personal or family connections. Such a conclu-sion does not suggest the way forward for younger respondents and their embedded ethnic networks are clear-cut, instead the younger generation is a religious-ethnic community negotiating the parameters of their relationship with community members and even the wider society.

The second generation of British South Asians in the West are in a unique position to carve out their identity in a much more proactive manner than their parents and this has implications for the resources they can draw upon for the business. However, it may be that the younger generation has not completely dispensed with the traditional ways of doing business, for example the younger generation talked about their involvement with social and religious events located within their ethnic networks. Researchers exploring the effects of migration on ethnic communities have emphasised how traditional customs and events reinforce access to resources embedded within ethnic networks (Allen, 1971; Ballard and Hurst, 1994). It is likely the younger generation still utilise these ethnic events in a similar way to their parents, that is as a means of generating contacts and reinforcing their networks but are perhaps not conscious of their behaviour. This can be explained by the distinction of the younger generation between their personal networks and business resources. This shift in attitude towards ethnic resources implies the unit of analysis for exploring ethnic networks has become more developed across both generations. Where previously the individual and business were considered as the same unit when exploring ethnic networks, it is possible to identify a divergence between the business and founder or successor and their networks.

Certain cases illustrated how the older generation had 'delegated' business networking to other employees or younger successors whilst older respondents still retained close personal networks within the ethnic community. This practice seemed to be even more prevalent amongst the younger respondents who clearly differentiated their networks between work and personal, ethnic and non-ethnic. All of this seems to imply when considering the nature of networking relationships, and more interestingly the notion of social capital, the basic unit of analysis has now split between the founder (or successor) and the business itself. This concept requires further exploration, but its potential has significant implications, if as seems to be the case, the younger generation continues to reinforce the distinction between themselves and the business. The benefit of this approach may enable the younger generation to draw upon resources of the ethnic community without necessarily experiencing the negative aspects often argued to hold back the development of the business (Sanders and Nee, 1987). Furthermore, this approach may enable the sustainability of the ethnic community over the longer-term as the younger generation invest in the network in a more conscious manner emphasising the beneficial aspects of involvement rather than ethnic networks facing eventual extinction.

Involvement of family members

The final research area of this thesis assessed the role of the mother as a buffer between both generations. The role of mothers, and indeed females, has been highlighted as an area that is seriously under-researched in the family business field. Existing work on female involvement in business has tended to focus on the hidden and exploitative nature of their participation which is particularly emphasised in ethnic-based businesses (Ram and Holliday, 1993; Marshack, 1994; Baines and Wheelock, 1998; Dhaliwal, 1998). The role of the mother has been acknowledged as a critical resource and often hidden but acknowledged to be very important and perhaps not as exploited as previously suggested. In order to assess attitudes towards female involvement the data collection focused on the perceptions of active family members towards the role and contribution of the wife (also the mother of the heir). This unorthodox approach to understanding the role of the wife presented an unusual approach of understanding family dynamics but more importantly illustrated how recognised active family members assessed the involvement of more 'latent' family members. Where female members are critical to the development of the business, if their involvement is largely ignored by key family members, their influence will be severely limited and is likely to go unnoticed over significant periods of time. As a result what is a crucial resource within the business can be neglected and may eventually result in complete decline.

The cases illustrated how respondents generated various perceptions to the involvement of wives (and mothers) in both business and personal relationships. The roles adopted by mothers were positioned along a continuum ranging from active involvement on a daily basis to no involvement in the business at all. With the exception of the final category, the remaining classifications presented opportunities for the mother to act as a buffer in some form between the generations. The research in this book builds on the notion of the mother as a buffer (Janjuha-Jivraj, 2004b). The buffer within this context presented the mother as the pivotal point between the two generations, often father and son, ensuring constant communication, particularly during disagreements. This meant extending her domestic role into the business, often in a very informal manner. The informality of this role also underpins its strength, as the older respondents recognised the influence of the wives in their dynamics with the younger generation more often than not they attempted to control this influence. In a number of cases the older respondents consciously maintained business discussions at work rather than allowing work to be discussed openly at home. By reinforcing this behaviour the older respondents were very clearly attempting to move the business away from the integrated family business approach towards the two areas between the founder and the business. This observation regarding the control of power draws the discussion back to questioning how to define the unit of analysis within family firms – should it be limited to the founder (and/or successor) and the business or should it be widened to incorporate the family and even influences from the ethnic network. As discussed earlier, the family business research field is moving away from the polarised view of the family and business towards a more integrated approach. Work by Wheelock and Oughton (1996) argued that research on familial labour within business should consider the household as a more useful unit of analysis rather than the single individual (entrepreneur or owner). Such an approach enables researchers to understand the resources available to the business from a variety of sources, not only limited to the social capital of the entrepreneur. Therefore, if the older respondents are consciously distancing the business from the very sources of support that helped its initial development and growth, one could argue this behaviour could potentially affect the longer-term survival of the business. Another issue also needs to be briefly considered at this stage within the context of mothers as buffers – the perception of exploitation.

Working dynamics across the generations

The dynamics of working relationships across generations in family businesses are influenced by a broad cross section of factors. The cultural background of the family creates the context in which the founder operates as an entrepreneur and hence influences the development and shape of the business. Whilst it is reasonable to argue that many of the examples in this book did not begin with the intention of becoming family dynasties, the founders did expect to draw upon the resources of the family, primarily through unpaid labour and emotional support. Researchers have argued social capital derived from family members is both critical and advantageous to enterprise development, but it also has drawbacks both for the scope of the business and the personal development of individuals who are involved in the business.

Existing research that focuses on the working dynamics of both generations in a family business has typically concentrated on the antagonistic relationship that develops between the father and the son (Levinson, 1971; Dyck *et al.*, 1999). Other work has focused on different permeations of the working dynamics by exploring the relationship between father and daughter (Dumas, 1989), mother and daughter (1992) and also siblings (Kuratko, 1995). The cases in this book illustrate how familial culture represents a critical factor in the working dynamics that develop between generations. Familial dynamics present a stronger case than previously for greater integration between the family and business in terms of research approaches.

10
Development of Family Firms over the Longer Term

Introduction

This chapter draws on the findings and conclusions from the research presented in the previous chapters to present a perspective on succession amongst Asian family firms. The approach constantly adopted in this book has been to understand the interaction of business, family (both immediate and wider) and the co-ethnic community in the context of family business succession. The countries identified for this research represent the Asian community in different stages of settlement and development which is an important part of the debate on family business survival and in particular the involvement of the younger generation from migrant-ethnic communities.

Family businesses present the most complex form of organisation in addition to operating within the multi-layered business environment, their size dictates the extent to which they are likely to be affected by shifts in the marketplace (i.e. the smaller the organisation the bigger the impact of market forces). The involvement of family members in the business creates a paradox for all involved. Business is considered essentially a rational, logical and objective activity where emotions are controlled and personal relationships develop within the context of the business. On the other hand the family is bound together by deep-seated complex emotions, there is not an easy get-out clause for members and thinking is more likely to be subjective and emotional with bonds of loyalty overriding logical thought processes. This contradictory existence for family business has long been acknowledged as a critical source of tension by researchers (Ward, 1987). The three-ringed model (Taiguri and Davis, 1982) clearly demonstrates how the intersection of these areas has implications for the working of both the business and the family. The development of the community-contextualised model for Asian family firms (Figure 4.2) emphasises the implications of kinship and the way in which different cultures influence the definition of what constitutes a family. Most of the research in the field of family business succession has adopted a typical approach to defining the family in terms of the immediate nuclear family, father, mother and children. The cases in this book highlight the impact of extended family members even across generations, in addition co-ethnic community members who are considered as kin can also be found to have a profound effect on the workings of such businesses. This approach questions the 'unit of currency' when dealing with family firms, an issue debated by Wheelock and Oughton (1996) in their review of what resources are consumed during entrepreneurship. As the family business field identifies more permeations in what constitutes familial involvement, often these differences will arise from research based on diverse case studies, particularly in terms of ethnicity and cultural background.

In spite of a shared ethnic background the cases in this book illustrate how migration to different geographical areas, and degrees of settlement along with adapting to different socio-economic contexts, creates different opportunities and working practices for communities. The family businesses in the case studies illustrate varied opportunities both in terms of individuals responding to market conditions and building on their own resources to generate enterprises. A common thread throughout the case studies has been the emphasis on education amongst the younger generation; there is an undeniable link between the level of education amongst a migrant community and the range of resources it generates. However, as the cases illustrate high levels of education have not obliterated entrepreneurial activity within this community.

This chapter presents a summary of the state of family firms in each of the countries – Kenya, the United Kingdom and the United States of America – before turning to the implications of these findings on the field of family business research.

The Kenyan experience

Amongst these cases there were greater instances of the younger respondents exhibiting varying degrees of filial obligation for entry into the family business. As the Kenyan businesses were established family firms having experienced inter-generational transition from first to second generation and embarking on second to third transition, the family were more likely to expect younger family members to join the business. In these cases there was strong evidence of the younger generation being groomed to join the business and not developing personal career choices contrary to familial expectations. The impact of grooming and expectations on the younger generation meant families placed a great deal of emphasis on the tradition of maintaining familial practices and traditions for both personal and business needs. The notion of expected filial obligation was particularly evident as many of the younger generation had been sent overseas for their university education. These experiences and qualifications opened many opportunities for the younger generation, which meant, unlike their parents, entry into the family business was not their only viable career route. Second-generation Kenyan respondents talked about their experiences of being forced into the business in order to fulfil familial expectations. For many older respondents this forced entry had caused some resentment on the lack of opportunities they faced to develop their own personal careers. This frustration became particularly more acute when many of the cases completed their transition from first to second generation leaving family members fractured and one-time partners now competing against each other. Many of the older respondents were adamant not to repeat these experiences by forcing their children into similar difficulties; ironically, however, a number of the younger Kenyan respondents still felt they were cajoled into joining the family business.

The younger Kenyan respondents who had the education and work experience from another country before deciding to return to the family business in Kenya were in a much stronger position than previous generations. First, the younger generation had the experience of working in subordinate positions in an external environment developing their work ethics and professionalism. These new skills were then transposed to the family business through their subsequent involvement. The introduction of new working practices initiated by the entry of the younger generation was not something previously experienced within the family business arena as many of the second-generation respondents had entered the business having completed their schooling at sixteen or eighteen. Whilst the entrance of the younger generation heralded the way to improved competitiveness and even better working conditions for lower level staff their settlement into the businesses still generated tensions and problems, as will be discussed in the next paragraph. The discussion on filial obligation in Chapter 8 generated different approaches to classifying filial obligation and, more importantly, explored how the nature of business entry impacted on the subsequent working relationships that developed between the generations. Business transition from the first to second generation reinforced the strong patriarchal nature of the Kenyan families, which meant the third generation who joined the business due to 'anticipated' filial obligation were entering a very strong traditional environment. In some cases the younger generation had to contend with not only the centrality of the founder but also the omnipresence of the grandfather, the founder of the business. Amongst the cases where the younger generation chose to return to the business based on their own choice ('unanticipated' filial obligation) as expected, the working relationship between both generations was slightly more balanced.

The Kenyan cases generated an unexpected element in the working position of the younger generation, on the whole generational relationships in these cases were harmonious and had developed into a good working dynamic. Some of the younger respondents faced considerable opposition to their entry into the business, not from older or other family members but from long-standing members of staff. These were individuals who had been with the business for a very long time, in some cases during its start-up. As highlighted in Chapter 9, the Kenyan cases had progressed further along their life cycle and along with an increased market share these businesses also developed their internal management structures. As the organisation of these businesses became more formalised there was a need to recruit non-family staff into senior management positions. When the second generation had joined the business non-family staff welcomed their entry as a sign of continuity and stability as the business would remain under family control. However, when the third generation joined the business, non-family staff did not feel the same need for family stability as senior positions were occupied by a variety of individuals and family continuity was not the necessary factor for the survival of the business. The senior positions of non-family staff along with significant periods of time and experience accumulated by these individuals meant the third-generation respondents often experienced challenges to their right to enter the business, particularly when they were on the fast track to managerial positions. The cases illustrate different examples of how these tensions were resolved, in the more extreme cases the solutions led to the resignation of non-family staff and in some cases the temporary withdrawal of the third generation. The experiences of the Kenyan cases highlight norms and practices which exist in family firms, notably the automatic assumption of control passing along blood lines can be challenged by non-family members. Whilst control is still retained by family members, dissatisfaction of non-family staff can undermine the performance of the business threatening its performance and ultimately its survival. When the second generation joined the business it was generally accepted by all stakeholders that they would enter managerial positions and eventually assume control of the business. Over time this automatic right to control the business by virtue of blood ties has been eroded by the elevation and greater democratisation within the business.

Experiences of family splits during the first-generational transition left deep rifts not only within the business, but also amongst family members and caused wider ripple effects within the ethnic embedded networks of the founders. Most of the second-generation Kenyan respondents had first-hand experience of these splits as conflicts between their uncles and fathers caused splits amongst the next generation of cousins. These experiences made the second generation determined not to repeat previous mistakes, and so they invested resources into identifying the best options for the future harmonious survival of the business and family through attendance at Business School family business courses. The impact of these courses extended beyond the family. Just as negative consequences of family businesses cause a ripple effect so too can positive actions. The individuals who had attended these courses were also prominent members of their ethnic networks and were able to disseminate the information to other family businesses within their network. The chain effect of this information enabled subsequent businesses to explore a wider range of options for second- to third-generational succession. Many of these businesses had adopted a strategic approach to succession that entailed a move away from the traditional behaviour of ownership and management being located within the family. Instead many of the businesses had implemented a strategic plan to separate these two retaining family control but recruiting non-family individuals to senior positions within the organisation. Analysis of the cases indicates the notion of separation of ownership and management is the next logical step for these businesses. This approach is the only way in which the various stakeholders and their interests within the business can be managed to enable the business to survive third-generational transition. Separation of ownership and management is not a novel concept within family firms, yet it is an idea that is not considered a natural fit with Asian family firms. This research has highlighted, however, that Asian businesses moving from second to third generation are facing similar problems to those experienced by other family businesses regardless of cultural background, and such an approach will become more acceptable over time. The challenge is to encourage the founders of businesses to consider separation of ownership and management as a viable option, rather than experiencing a traumatic succession risking further family and business splits, which in turn risks destabilising the economic strength of both the family and the ethnic community.

Kenyan firms faced the slow but inevitable erosion of the successor pool. An overriding factor that underpins the continuation of these Asian businesses is the wider political and economic instability of Kenya. The cases in this book have illustrated how Asian firms in this environment have maintained family involvement due to a combination of internal micro factors; anticipated filial obligation as well as macro circumstances; external employment opportunities in Kenya offer very limited scope for advancement.

The British experience

The motivations for starting up a business amongst the British cases were varied, but more often than not, the root cause originated from a need to establish a secure financial base for the family. However, beyond this was perhaps an implicit need to develop a source from which the individual could hold a position of 'status' within their professional and social circle, perhaps even recreating what they had experienced in East Africa or in the Indian sub-continent. The negative and positive factors associated with entrepreneurial activity, and in particular ethnic activity, have been explored in great detail throughout this book. Reliance on social capital enables founders to draw upon personal resources during the start-up and development of the business, often these resources are derived from close personal contacts and family. Working patterns of Asian family firms therefore indicate that these businesses are not conducive to involving external individuals in positions of senior management. This behaviour is likely to be applicable to all family firms, however the cultural background and experiences of the British Asian community reinforced ethnic solidarity amongst the older migrant respondents. Analysis of the younger British respondents illustrates the impact of wider socio-economic integration across the different aspects of their lives. Attitudes of the younger generation indicate they are more amenable to welcoming non-family members and non-Asians into positions of senior management. The critical issue entails both generations moving towards this approach of considering non-family resources. The implication of achieving this is nothing short of a paradigm shift amongst the older generation.

The demise of potential heirs facing Kenyan Asian family firms also affects British Asian family firms. The impact of these conditions have been addressed at various points in this book; however, the end result of such insecurity is the greater pooling of resources into the family thus increasing and strengthening its social capital. As Britain does not have similar macro-economic and social conditions to Kenya, the younger generation of Asians find they have a wider number of opportunities available to them when considering career prospects. The wider choice of options available to the younger generation enables them to consciously decide if they wish to join the family business, although this research has illustrated there is still evidence of business entry through anticipated filial obligation. The findings in this research highlight entry into the business is not usually a straightforward emotional attachment to creating or maintaining a family dynasty. Most of the cases showed both generations considering the options available to the younger generation, external career opportunities and the longer-term viability of the business to remain as a family business and achieve growth to accommodate other family members.

The British cases in this research came from a variety of industrial sectors and varied considerably in their sizes. The businesses that were either classified as medium enterprises or displayed the potential for growth usually had a strong sense of anticipated filial obligation. The cases where growth was not the primary intention of the business represented reluctance on either (or both) generation to automatically initiate filial entry – in these cases unexpected events triggered the entry of the younger generation. The most significant example of long-term aspirations and younger generation entry was perhaps illustrated by examples where the younger generation forced their way into the business. The businesses had reached a stage of settlement without growth, this was fine for the older generation, as they had no need to accommodate the next generation of family members. However, the entry of the younger generation initiated a catalytic effect whereby businesses were suddenly forced upon a rapid growth trajectory in order for them to become a viable entity to sustain the next generation. This research has found for the time being businesses with the potential for growth are likely to remain attractive options for younger family members as a career choice. However, whether this is likely to continue to the third generation of British Asians remains to be seen.

The traditional approach to heirs has been along male lines, this is applicable to family firms in general, regardless of their ethnic background. Women have consistently played an important role in the cases across all three countries, however their impact has been particularly highlighted in the UK examples. Wives of founders (also mothers of heirs) were identified to contribute to the family business in more covert ways, rather than the traditional forms of unpaid labour. They occupied a critical position in maintaining harmonious relationships between both generations working together in the business – the buffer role. This role reinforces the notion of domestic roles carrying over into the business environment and can also be argued to be somewhat exploitative due to lack of acknowledgement of her involvement in managing the business. The counter-argument to this proposition suggests the central and hidden role of the mother provides the basis of strength, which allows her to be very effective in her role as an intermediary between the generations. As illustrated by the cases, often the 'active' family members were unaware of how they were using the mother in their relationships with other family members for business purposes.

Daughters provide an interesting area in the field of family business succession. They are part of the group highly neglected in the body of research, however this is underpinned by their lack of involvement in the family business field. The disengagement of daughters from family firms is not necessarily ethnic-specific, however certain cultural traits of Asian migrant communities are likely to reinforce the invisibility of daughters (along with other female members). The few cases both in the United Kingdom and Kenya with the involvement of daughters illustrated how they were a hidden gem and their performance in the business not only exceeded familial expectations, but was a real benefit to the business. The examples in these cases also emphasise the difficulties the daughters faced due to their gender, particularly in terms of asserting their authority within the business. Daughters provide a new source of successor, they have the educational skills, often the external work experience and bring a different dynamic to the much-cited antagonistic father–son working relationship (Dumas, 1992). Their impact on future family businesses cannot be underestimated.

The American experience

The migrants in the United States were the most recent arrivals amongst all of those studied for this book. They had learnt from the experiences of their community members who had migrated ten, twenty or thirty years earlier. They also had the benefits of settling into an environment that was largely more welcoming to Asian migrants and a society that actively encouraged entrepreneurship. The American cases presented a different perspective on younger generation entry into the business. Filial obligation still played an important role in family business entry, however the means of entry and the ensuing nature of working relationship between the generations were much more smooth and less extreme in the volatility of emotions. As with the British cases self-employment provided a route for the migrants to achieve stability and settlement for themselves and their families. The businesses were not created with the intention of becoming dynasties, instead they were expected to enable the younger family members to continue and complete their education. The younger members had flexibility in their future choice of careers that also encompassed the possibility of self-employment outside of the family firm.

The trend amongst the younger generation was to enter the family business and also develop their own businesses sometimes with the involvement of other family members not involved in the main family firm. This dual aspect to their business activities undoubtedly influenced the working relationship between the generations. The entry of the younger generation into the business had been quite smooth and a natural result of business expansion requiring family-based manpower. As the younger generation created their own businesses they also built up their own credibility as entrepreneurs that helped to establish authority amongst family and non-family members in the business. In addition, in starting their own businesses with other family members the sons were able to draw upon familial resources that would have been typically neglected by their parents – their sisters and even partners, wives and fiancés.

Resources drawn from family have created opportunities for growth in the businesses. This is not new but is pertinent to ethnic migrant communities. The businesses in the American cases illustrate high growth activity and the development of chains through franchising activity. In general these types of businesses, namely gas stations, fast food outlets, dollar stores and grocery stores require low skills and have relatively low non-financial barriers to entry, however the family owning the business are relatively protected by the brand names of the companies. This is likely to create a stronger and more secure base for the family and in turn create a business that is attractive for younger generation involvement.

The American cases have not yet experienced inter-generational transition, they are in the initial stages of preparation but have not progressed as far as the British cases. In most of the Kenyan cases that had experienced at least the first round of inter-generational succession this had led to family splits and ultimately personal rifts. Time will tell whether the UK- and USA-based cases will face similar casualties, inevitably there will be family conflicts and the fallout from tensions during inter-generational succession, however the younger family firms have the opportunity to learn from the experiences of others.

One of the key outcomes from the Kenyan cases to ensure a greater chance of survival has been the emphasis on separation of ownership and management within such firms. This scenario usually means family members retain ownership of the business but do not have active daily involvement in the operations of the business. By adopting this approach the family and the business have clearer lines of delineation and are therefore less likely to have the conflicts that arise due to inter-action of rational and emotional units. In addition it is more common for firms in the West to prepare for the future through the provisions of wills, this does place more emphasis on the tax aspects of transition rather than managerial provisions, but it does however create some foundation for transfer of ownership.

Implications for further research in the field of family firms

This research has focused exclusively on family firms in different areas of the South Asian Diaspora. The findings generated from the case studies identify a number of trends that are common to these businesses regardless of their location. Some of these trends are pertinent to all family firms in spite of different ethnic backgrounds, however the cultural contexts of the businesses provide unique backdrops in the way family members respond to challenges that are specific to family firms. The approach to family firms continuously emphasises the importance of the crossover between the family and the business and the implications of this on how individuals in these areas manage their relationships. When researching Asian family firms the collective culture requires the three-ringed circle model developed by Taiguri and Davis (1982) to extend the influential bodies to include extended family members and members of the co-ethnic community. The cultural background of the family and the business has a significant impact on the way in which the family unit is defined. Considerable energy has been invested by a variety of researchers into defining the family firm

(Shanker and Astrachan, 1996; Carsud *et al.*, 1997; Westhead and Cowling, 1998), however it is equally important to have a clear understanding of what constitutes the family. The family unit can be broadened to include extended family members and even co-ethnic community members, in short anyone who is considered kin. Involvement in the family business is not always a clear precursor to inclusion in the family business arena as the nature of engagement in the business may be covert and/or infrequent. As the field of family business succession expands to incorporate a broader perspective of ethnic differences, greater attention needs to be payed to these cultural factors.

The cultural patterns of these communities are not static, they are continuously evolving in response to wider societal changes as well as the progression and development of the younger generation. This is particularly true of daughters, who have been highlighted as an untapped significant resource for family firms. As a whole the field of family firms has been primarily focused on male family members, creating a vacuum on research with women as the central focus. This gap has also been identified by researchers in the family business field (Martin, 2005) and provides a route for research into a new field of the dynamics of family relationships.

The field of family business research is buoyant in the United States with synergistic links between academics and practitioners, consultants and professional services (lawyers, accountants). The United Kingdom lags behind the United States in this field, providing an opportunity for growth in both research and professional services. In Kenya most research and business support attention focuses on native African businesses (Bewayo, 1997). Asian businesses are virtually hidden in terms of state-support provisions and even academic research. There is little existing research on Asian family firms in Kenya (Janjuha-Jivraj and Woods, 2001), however these businesses provide an opportunity for subsequent family firms in other countries to reduce the likelihood of deep family rifts and conflicts by providing examples of successful and also unsuccessful generational transition.

This book provides an international perspective of migrant South Asian family business communities and draws out the complexities of the relationships and positions of the key stakeholders. Some of the issues discussed in this book are not unique to Asian family firms nor are the solutions, whilst other issues are ethnic-specific and may evaporate with successive generations or continue depending on their perceived benefits to the business and the family. The international dimension of the cases illustrates important key similarities in the way

Asians families and business operate, regardless of their background; the links and bonds that sustain communities across countries have also provided important routes for trading and exploiting business opportunities. Time will tell whether these bonds will maintain their commercial viability and remain integral to the development of South Asian family firms.

Appendix 1: Kenyan Cases

Case K1

	K1	
Industry	Food Manufacturing	
Year established	1954	
Founder	Father of K1a	
Employee size	200	

	K1a	K1b
Relationship	Father	Son
Age	46–55	25–34
Business position	Chair	Director
Year of entry	1969	1995
Educational qualifications	'A' Levels	Degree
Previous employment	×	×

The business in this case study was one of the pioneering firms in the field of food manufacturing across East Africa. The business had been started by K1a's father and was now in the third generation of family management. K1a had been groomed to join the business from a very young age, he felt trapped by this approach and had tried to ensure the same fate did not happen to his son. However K1b also grew up from a young age with the knowledge that he was expected to join the family firm. This emanated from his grandfather and other family members. Both generations expressed their disappointment with career options limited to the family business.

When K1a joined the business he was aware that a number of people regarded him as privileged and considered his entry the result of nepotism. When he joined he had difficulty managing relations in the business as his uncles who were involved resented his entrance. As he was the eldest member of the next generation he was the first to join the business and this created territorial concerns amongst his uncles for their children's rights in the business.

The situation between the uncles and K1a was very difficult; however, he persevered until their departure from the business and Kenya in the early 1970s. K1b experienced his own challenges in establishing himself in the business; however, it was senior staff rather than family members who put a resistance to his entrance. The general manager was unhappy with K1b's entrance and they had conflicts about most aspects of the business. The only way K1b felt he could resolve the situation was by leaving the company, which he did; however in the meantime his father identified problems with the general manager and decided not to renew his contract. After the general manager left the business underwent a complete restructuring programme and K1b returned to the organisation.

The experiences of K1a joining the business and the subsequent impact of K1b's entry into the business made the family far more reticent about encouraging further family members into the business. K1a had experienced the drawbacks of having too many members involved in the business and so he did not mind a great deal when his younger son chose not to join the business. K1a's wife had no involvement in the business on a formal level. K1a did, however, describe how his son used to involve the mother in the business, particularly when he disagreed with his father's decisions. K1a stood firm in ensuring his wife did not provide a conduit for his son and stopped her involvement. He also became determined to ensure business issues were not discussed at home, which also limited exposure of the business to non-active family members.

Both generations felt they had a good relationship with each other, as they emphasised the importance of trust and understanding. K1b however did feel his father had very high expectations that were sometimes difficult to fulfil. K1a felt working together had enabled both of them to get to know each other well, however it did create tensions that impacted their personal relationships. He felt it was far too difficult to separate the relationships between home and workplace. K1a also had to manage the influence of his father on the business and the relationship with K1b. He acknowledged that because his father was a pioneer in establishing the business he was willing to compromise in relations with family members both personally and in the workplace. K1b valued the relationship he had with his father, he was able to discuss issues in a frank manner but still deferred to his father's judgement in business decisions.

The longer-term vision for the business for both generations is a shift away from family control. This had been and agreed between father and son with a plan to grow the business for eventual floatation. In order to achieve this the business needed to undergo further management restructuring to ensure more non-family managers could be appointed to cover all aspects of the business. K1a was adamant the business would not become a burden for the family, however K1b was still keen for part of the business to remain under family control (e.g. through family shareholdings). For both the father and the son this view represented a much more objective approach compared to the emotional relationship between the business and the founder (the grandfather). However they were clear in their view of the business as a rational unit and they felt this did not provide a hindrance in planning for the future of the business and the family.

Case K2

	K2	
Industry	Dry Cleaning and Tourism	
Year established	1951	
Founder	Father of K2a	
Employee size	180	
	K2a	K2b
Relationship	Father	Daughter
Age	46–55	25–34
Business position	Chief Executive	Director
Year of entry	1976	1995
Educational qualifications	Degree	Degree
Previous employment	✓	✓

K2a's father began the family business as a dry cleaner in 1951. K2a was one amongst five brothers in the family, initially on completion of his education he joined the family business. His eldest brother was already involved in the business, having had to sacrifice his education; K2a was the next one to join but was able to complete his degree. The expectation in the family was that some family members would join the business, but each son was also encouraged to develop their own career paths as well. The business was open to the sons who had an interest in working there.

After K2a joined the business there were problems, in particular between his elder brother and father. During this time K2a left the business and got a job in a bank. He stayed there for six years before returning to the business. K2a returned to the business for a year and brokered the relationship between his father and brother before the latter decided to leave the business. The source of conflict between the father and brother lay in the amount of control delegated down. K2a's father was worried about his elder son's desire for more control and how this would affect the position of other family members, both those who subsequently joined the business as well as those who were not directly involved in the business but nonetheless beneficiaries. None of the other brothers joined the business and so K2a became the chief executive when his father retired.

K2b had a very different experience surrounding her entry into the family firm. She had travelled to Canada to study switching from natural sciences to social sciences. On completion of her education she accumulated varied employment experience in Canada including starting up her own export business. After a while she felt she had better opportunities back in Kenya for employment and a better standard of living. Prior to her move to Canada she had spent a year working in the family business and was put off by the experience. She had felt very restricted within the business and constrained as she would miss opportunities externally. However, on her return to Kenya she changed her mind. Her initial entrance into the business was a slow process. K2b spent time in every department of the business, including the production of hangers, answering the telephone, working in the shops and hotels. In addition she was given a project that she had to manage in order to prove her competence. Her parents had not expected her to enter the business, however both were pleased with her decision to return to Kenya and join her father.

When K2a joined the business the staff welcomed his entrance, they were very positive about the entrance of the next generation. Although there were initial anxieties about his impact on the business, they had a general sense the business would not undergo any radical overhauls. Many of the senior staff had been with the business for the last twenty years and shared the same ethics of hard work and loyalty as the family members. K2b found a very different scenario by the time she joined the business. Having experienced the process of initiation by working her way around the business K2b had to manage the sensitive issue of having power without snubbing senior management. In order to manage this her father, K2a, asked permission for her to hold areas of responsibility from senior management. This meant she also had to report to senior management, and this was generally received well by the staff. However, there was resistance from some of the long-serving staff who were unhappy about her involvement in the business. K2a felt a lot of this was due to her gender. Her brother joined the business after her and found that within five months of joining he had become a director. Within the company she found her brother had far more credibility instantly than she did because of his sex. It also had implications outside of the business to when suppliers expressed a preference to deal with a man rather than a woman, over time they managed to resolve this. K2b and her brother have developed a close working relationship, however they had to work hard to ensure negative reactions of employees and other stakeholders to working with a woman do not affect the effectiveness of their fraternal relationship. In addition whilst K2b feels she has a good working relationship with her father, she is aware of the generational difference and the impact this has particularly with a daughter in senior position in the family firm. This is all the more clearer by experiences of the previous generation; her aunt (father's sister) never had the option to join the business.

The family had a clear method for dealing with personal and working relationships. They would hold regular weekly meetings on a Monday evening to discuss issues that had crossed over from family into the business and vice versa. In general the family rule had been personal problems remain at home and work problems should be dealt with at work, however the grey area of crossover is dealt with in these family councils. K2a described this as an opportunity to deal with emotional baggage rather than letting it fester over time. He was very keen to try this approach as he did not want a repetition of the relationship he had experienced between his father and elder brother. Although initially it had been difficult to begin these sessions and encourage and also accept the emotions over time, K2a has seen a difference in the way family members deal with each other both in terms of their personal and working lives.

The openness of this relationship has manifested itself in shared long-term plans for the business across both generations. K2a has talked about retirement, his plan to withdraw from the business and dedicate more of his time to charity and voluntary interests. He has been keen to leave the business for some time. K2b concurs with this, she and her brother are aware K2a would like to leave the business over the next five years but they are keen for him to stay involved for longer. K2a is keen for the business to eventually restructure so that it is owned by the family but managed by external professionals. Under K2a's leadership the business has experienced significant growth and diversification providing a lot of opportunities for K2b and her brother. Within this K2b and her brother may choose to maintain the business as it is or even separate sections and run them independently. Both agree recruitment is a critical issue for the future of the business.

Case K3

	K3	
Industry	Wholesale distributors of electrical appliances	
Year established	1954	
Founder	Father of K3a	
Employee size	135	

	K3a	K3b
Relationship	Father	Son
Age	55–64	25–34
Business position	Chairman	Director
Year of entry	1975	1990
Educational qualifications	Masters	Masters
Previous employment	✓	×

The business in this case study was initially purchased by K3a's father in a smaller format. K3a's father was able to develop the business and create a large wholesale-based business for the construction and service industries. Gradually K3a and his three brothers all joined the business. The brothers had different working styles and found this did not lend itself to a productive and harmonious working environment. One by one K3a's brothers decided to leave the business, one left Kenya and migrated to Canada. The other two brothers decided to withdraw from business, but retain their involvement as silent partners whilst running their own separate businesses. K3a had always been the dominant manager and so he remained in the business by buying out most of his brothers' shares. The expectation had been that K3a and his brothers would all join the business and enable it grow through their manpower and resources. However there were power struggles amongst the siblings, by the time K3a joined his brother was already established in the organisation. They had different expectations for the business, K3a was keen for the business to grow through opening up more branches, his brother however wanted to maintain the status quo. By this time their father had passed away and the tension that arose from these differences led to the older brother leaving the business.

The experiences of familial involvement in the business did not induce K3a to encourage his son's involvement in the business. K3b had not been groomed nor had he experienced any expectations to join the family firm. After his 'A' levels he was not sure what field he wanted to specialise in, although he had an interest in the business. He spent a year working in the business before deciding to continue with his studies focusing on Finance and Management for his undergraduate and postgraduate qualifications in the United Kingdom. After his Masters her returned to Kenya and joined the family business. By this time he felt ready to join the business and was confident that he would be able to contribute something to the organisation and also develop his own skills. By the time K3b joined the business his father was the only other family member involved and so he did not have to deal with the same tensions experienced by his father.

K3a still involves his brothers in the business through weekly updates. Major decisions are made by K3a, along with his two brothers, who are partners, and his son, K3b. K3a's wife has no involvement in the business although she is involved in the discussions that often occurred at home. When K3b first joined the business K3a found his wife would often take to her son's side in father–son disputes. K3a discouraged this and over time managed to separate home and work by limiting business discussions at home. The relationship between K3a and K3b was fine, however there were problems in attitudinal differences towards money. K3a felt his son was more extravagant in his expenditure for the business, he attributed this to the different experiences they had whilst growing up. Although K3a highlighted this as a problem he was still keen to ensure his son had the opportunity to try out new ideas and not feel constrained within the business. Their working relationship was maintained by a clear distinction of responsibilities, with K3b in charge of the branches and therefore the final decision-maker in this respect. K3b echoed his father's sentiments by acknowledging differences in the way they approached the business, however he felt their relationship was sufficiently strong that they were able to talk about things openly. He also identified a disparity in their approaches to money and investments in marketing and creating the business image.

K3a was sensitive to the delicate nature of their relationship, emphasising the importance of maintaining a professional approach in a relationship heavily embedded in parent–child emotions. He was very clear about the different influences on each of them and in particular the implications of education on shaping his son. Drawing on his own experiences of University and referring back to the relationships with his family he argued that educating children meant they would come back with their own ideas and expectations.

The relationship between father and son was perhaps one of the more complex relationship in this collection of cases. The father clearly described the mechanics and ideal ways to manage the relationship, however his emotions meant it was still very difficult to let go. This was very evident in their plans for the future of the business. K3a had made informal plans for retirement, however his son did not think he would ever completely leave the business, as it is too important to him. K3b's plans for the business included the recruitment of external professional managers and a developed management structure that would enable the business to move away from family influence. He anticipated he would be the last family member to be actively involved in the management of the business and hoped the organisation would evolve into a form that enabled family members to take on directorships (separation of ownership and management). K3a's expectations for the business were less clear. He wanted the business to become more professional, however he was unclear about how this could be achieved. His desire was for the business to succeed to the fourth generation and acknowledged this required investment from non-family shareholders. He talked about giving incentives to long-standing senior staff but again details were not clear. His desire was to maintain the focus of the business and not consider diversification in case it was not successful. K3b was keen to try new markets and ideas, in his view the business needed to adapt to the environment rather than remain as dinosaurs.

Appendix 2: British Cases

Case B1

	B1	
Industry	Food Processing	
Year established	1973	
Founder	B1a	
Employee size	23 full-time staff	
	B1a	**B1b**
Relationship	Father	Son
Age	46–55	25–34
Business position	Director	Director
Year of entry	1973	1994
Educational qualifications	Diploma	Masters
Previous employment	✓	✓

The business is a food processing company specialising in Indian ingredients and spices. The father (B1a) came to Britain in 1964 from Tanzania. His intention was to complete his studies and return home, however the problems in East Africa did not encourage him to return and so he decided to settle in Britain. On the completion of his studies (Diploma in Business and Management) he worked in the Management Accounts department of a factory. However he was faced with limited employment opportunities and the responsibilities of fatherhood providing the stimulus to leave his job. He started up the business with three partners, none of whom were family members. The business began as a small-scale import business focusing on limited spices that could be sold to the migrant Asian community in Britain. The partners subsequently left the business. By this time B1a's cousins had joined the business and the increased manpower enabled the business to grow considerably. B1a's wife was also involved in the business, with a particular role in marketing the business through developing associated products, such as recipe books, and attending exhibitions.

B1a had not expected his son to join the business. The family expectation was that B1b would complete his education and get a professional job. However, B1a's wife suffered severe illness which meant she had to withdraw from the business. Around this time the business also split, as family members wanted to separate out. B1a retained control of the business having bought out other family members. And along with his cousin the other individuals who were consulted about the business were his wife and father (the latter being based in

India). B1a remained in the business with his cousin, however B1a needed extra support as his wife's illness meant he was constantly away from the business for a long time. No other family member was willing or available to provide the necessary manpower support to run the business. By this time B1b had finished his degree and been offered a job in the city in Investment Banking, however he decided to defer his entry into the job in order to support the business. He had experience of working in the business whilst growing up, mainly involved in the overseas business plants.

Despite the expectations of B1b to create his own professional career there were no strong reactions from family members when he entered the business. His father felt guilty that perhaps he was missing out on opportunities to develop his own career and follow his peers, however B1b was adamant he wanted to remain in the business. Non-family employees did not have a significant reaction to his entrance either, however he was aware that he needed to build up his credibility with clients. The business he had entered worked on long-standing relationships with suppliers and customers both in Britain and abroad. He needed to invest his resources into the business in order to ensure he built up a good track-record with business contacts so that they would be willing to work with him directly, rather than through his father. In many ways the absence of B1a to look after his wife accelerated B1b's involvement in the business. He had to take on responsibilities at a much faster rate than would have been the case had his father been present in the business on a daily basis. This enabled B1b to build up his experience and balance the option of remaining in the business or taking up the city job. Although he tried to balance the two, he decided he had invested far more in the business and could not afford to walk away.

B1b's decision to remain in the business enabled family members in senior positions to think more strategically about the long-term development of the business over the next five years. In the meantime as the mother recovered B1a returned to the business, his wife however did not. Both B1a and his wife had decided they would remain in the background now that B1b had committed to the business. Father and son developed a close working relationship. B1b's accelerated responsibility in the business and his father's sense of gratitude and guilt towards his son created a more harmonious working relationship. B1a described their relationship as colleagues rather than as father and son. This enabled B1b to challenge business decisions made by his father. B1a found himself in a difficult position, his wife did not understand the openness of the relationship he had with B1b and she reacted angrily when his son argued with him. B1a adopted an approach to encourage greater openness both in his management style and opportunities for the business. He described how at times he was not sure about his son's plans for the business, but felt he had to be fair and try new ideas that seemed appropriate. At the same time, however, he also had to contend with his father back in India who was still an important stakeholder in the business. Despite the physical distance, B1a's father still had a regular input in the development of the business. At times these ideas conflicted with those of B1b, and B1a found himself in the difficult position of trying to keep both his son and father satisfied.

B1a felt the relationship with his son has improved a great deal and is based on respect for his achievements. He also acknowledged he had to give B1b the freedom to try out new thinking in the business (many of which have been successful) otherwise B1b would have left. B1b agreed with his father's perspective on the relationship. He recognised his father had given him the freedom to implement changes very early on in his involvement in the business. He also accepted that he had a tendency to dominate issues that he felt very passionate about, however over time both he and his father have developed a monitoring structure that requires decisions to be delegated to professional (external) managers in line with business expansion.

Both father and son have discussed future plans for the business, informally. B1a has discussed a time frame for retirement. However both generations feel that time is some years away. B1b still needs to learn more about the business, particularly the linkages and improving his relationships with overseas suppliers, B1a agrees with this. B1a is keen for the business to remain in family ownership over the longer term. They have received offers to sell the company which they have rejected. However B1b is keen to develop other career opportunities in the future. They have resolved these potentially conflicting desires by planning a move towards a state of separation of ownership and management for the business. However they are aware they need to keep building up the business in order to attract investors that could make the project viable.

Case B2

	B2	
Industry	Hotels	
Year established	1975	
Founder	B2a	
Employee size	180	
	B2a	**B2b**
Relationship	Father	Son
Age	46–55	<24
Business position	Director	General Manager
Year of entry	1984	1992
Educational qualifications	'O' Levels	'A' Levels
Previous employment	✓	×

This case is based in the tourism sector, operating hotels and restaurants across England, with a strong base in Central London. B2a migrated from Kenya in 1975 in order to have a more settled life in Britain. His family had a business in Kenya that he joined after completing his 'O' levels. However he felt there were better opportunities for him abroad and so decided to settle in Britain with his wife. Although he had his in-laws who were already in Britain he did not rely on them for support. Instead he found employment working in a hotel as a manager. Over the following nine years he built up the experience and resources to buy his own hotel. As the business grew he recruited his brother-in-law as an accountant for the business. The business had been established as a means of providing support for B2a and his family. Both B2a and his wife expected B2b to complete his education and become a professional. Initially it seemed this plan was working, B2b had completed his first year of Dentistry at university, however B2b was not enjoying the subject and decided to drop out. He had always wanted to be involved in the business and so a post-'A' level business- and economics-related course instead.

In the meantime B2a was planning early retirement. He expected B2b to complete his Dentistry degree and set up his own practice. B2a had started making plans to sell the business and retire in India with his wife. When B2b left his degree he pursued his desire to enter the family business. B2a was not happy about his son's decisions and was very reluctant to allow him to enter the business, he wanted his son to stand on his own feet and develop his own identity. However his wife was pleased their son wanted to work with his father and this influenced the final decision.

When B2a finally agreed to let his son join the business he ensured his son had to work hard to prove himself. The basis of entry for B2b was to take on the lease of a hotel. This meant B2b was responsible for the whole business, including paying rent for the hotel to his father. The rent was set a relatively high amount, as B2a was certain B2b would not be successful in making the payments along with the other costs of running the unit. To his surprise B2b not only paid the rent but also made extra money. During this time B2b relied on his uncle a great deal for support, partly because he was present more often than B2a and also because B2b did not want to show too much vulnerability to his father.

B2b was very young when he first joined the business. He felt staff (non-family) found it very difficult to take orders from someone who was a lot younger and also relatively inexperienced. He was also aware that a number of the staff remembered him as a small boy, which made it more challenging for him to assert himself. However through regular morning briefings he built up a rapport with the staff and was able to establish his rules and business operations. However the son felt a lot of people initially perceived him as being born with a silver spoon in his mouth, both from within and outside the company. He acknowledged that people were likely to feel jealous and see him doing little more than collecting money his father made. B2b felt some family members also had these feelings towards him, viewing his decisions as taking the easy option. B2a has been aware of the emotions towards his son. He acknowledged that it was difficult for staff when his son become the second most highly paid person in the company, however B2a felt this was justified by B2b's improvements to the business.

B2a made sure his son learnt not to trust everyone and was very careful, especially around family. Both individuals had a very limited and tight network of people they spoke to regarding business decisions, namely their spouses and the other family members involved in the business as well as each other. The relationship between B2a and B2b is one of the more complex dynamics amongst the cases in this book. The personal relationship between father and son had been quite temperamental, the insistence of B2b to join the business did very little to improve this. B2a resented his son's entrance into the business, particularly as this required him to revise his retirement strategy and reconfigure the business to ensure it had the potential to grow and become a viable opportunity for his son over the longer term. Although he had planned to eventually pass on the business to his son over time, he felt his son had forced him rather than allowing the father to do it when he wanted to. B2a's wife adopted the important role of mediator in the relationship. B2b described how when he first joined the business he relied on his mother a great deal for advice and support, particularly when he had problems with his father. Over time the mother maintained a more neutral position which B2b recognised, however he was also aware that she mediated a lot of conflicts in the relationship with his father. Working together has enabled both generations to develop a more open relationship and this brought them closer together. B2b felt the time they spent together at work was at the crux of improving their relationship. B2a maintained a dominant position in the business with final decision-making authority. He felt there was still a long way for his son to go in terms of development and awareness in the business environment.

In terms of business succession B2a has prepared a ten-year plan that covered both the financial and managerial aspects of succession. During this period B2a has sufficient time to groom B2b for the eventual handover of control. B2b was aware of his father's earlier plans for retirement, however he was not familiar with the amendments to these plans following his entrance into the business. Both generations intend to ensure the business remains under family ownership with some external investment. Details of management remaining in the business had not been discussed between the generations.

Case B3

	B3	
Industry	Catering	
Year established	1966	
Founder	B3a	
Employee size	400	
	B3a	**B3b**
Relationship	Father	Son
Age	46–55	25–34
Business position	Chair	Financial Controller
Year of entry	1975	1996
Educational qualifications	Diploma	Degree
Previous employment	✓	✓

This is the second case amongst the British cases that is based in the tourism and catering sector. B3a came to Britain to study in 1966, he had family members who were already in Britain when he came over, although he did not stay with them they helped him settle. Once he completed a Certificate in Business Administration he decided to stay on and start-up his own business. The motivation for this came from his desire to be independent, as he did not want to work for anyone else. He had the opportunity to use family resources to help him start-up his business. The first business was established in 1975 in the catering industry. As his sons grew up he was very keen to start-up a business that would become a family concern, he felt the involvement of family members would enable the business to grow. This expectation influenced university and career choices for B3b. His choice of degree was Accounting as B3b felt the subject would be beneficial to the business and also provided an insurance plan if involvement in the family business did not work out. After finishing university he worked in an Accountancy firm for four years before joining the family business. B3b entered the business at a management level; during this time, he learnt more about the business before becoming the financial controller. His experiences of working elsewhere along with his qualifications meant that he entered the business with credibility and so staff more readily accepted his position and authority.

Since then B3b's younger brother joined the business, the three individuals are the only family members involved in the business. B3a's wife has no involvement in the business and neither generation consulted her about the business either. The two brothers are both financial controllers with responsibility for separate divisions of the business.

The personal relationship between B3a and B3b is steady and provided a foundation for their working relationship. Within this dynamic B3a maintained the dominant position both in their personal and working relationships. He described how he resolved disagreements by making the final decision. This was the characteristic of their relationship throughout with B3a deciding the level of B3b's involvement and his son complying. As B3b spent more time working in the business he was able to assert himself over his areas of responsibility and thereby increase his level of control. However B3b still acknowledged his father's level of influence on the final say for important business-based decisions.

There are no plans for the retirement of B3a. B3b has acknowledged the business is far too important to his father for him to ever let go completely. B3a sees the business remaining in family control and under family management as well. Both generations expect business growth and potential diversification, all the more possible with three family members heading up separate areas. B3b seemed to be far more objective when discussing future options for the business compared to his father, however even within this he was adamant the business would remain under family control.

Appendix 3: American Cases

Case A1

	A1	
Industry	Gas station and fast food franchise	
Year established	1990	
Founder	A1a	
Employee size	20 full-time staff	
	A1a	**A1b**
Relationship	Father	Son
Age	45–54	Under 25
Business position	Director	Manager
Year of entry	1990	1997
Educational qualifications	None	Degree
Previous employment	Always in business	×

The family already had some association with the USA, A1a's father had been living in the USA for five years before returning to India. A1a, his brother and their respective families were successful in their applications to settle in the USA and following their move in 1990, A1a's father returned to the States two years later. Initially the family settled in New York however they soon moved to Kansas. The two brothers were looking for business opportunities whilst A1a's wife worked as a hotel chambermaid and supported the family. After a few months A1a received a phone call from a supplier who had a store for sale, the site was very run down and required considerable work to build it up to a suitable condition for trading. The brothers agreed to purchase the store and along with A1a's wife immersed themselves in building up the business. After three years A1a's brother left the business to start-up his own enterprise. The family kept investing in the business building on the initial site until they had created a chain of nine gas stations, mostly based in Kansas with a few in Dallas. In addition the family had also diversified into other retail-based businesses, including a convenience store.

As the business achieved stability and began to generate a steady income A1a's wife also became less involved in the business, by 1996 she had completely withdrawn from the business. The rationale for the wife's withdrawal from the business was her need to spend more time with the family and with the business generating sufficient income it was no longer necessary for her to work.

As A1b was growing up he had always had some involvement in the business. When his father and uncle started up the first gas station, thirteen-year-old A1b was drafted in to help out with general menial tasks. Two years later his involvement had been promoted to operating the cash tills and handling sales. At this stage he also started to receive a wage for his involvement in the business. By the time he was seventeen A1b was managing a few stores on his own. This role required overseeing the inventory, balancing the accounts and banking the takings. He was also included in decisions regarding the purchase of new units. In addition to his involvement in the family business A1b continued to study, initially he wanted to study Engineering but his exposure to the business led him into the field of economics and finance. He gained two degrees in Finance and Economics. Although A1b had some interest in developing his own career this was subsumed by his interest in the family business. He had never considered working elsewhere. His father had mixed reactions to A1b's involvement, although he was pleased to have him on board; he wanted A1b to develop a profession and continue his education to achieve this. However A1b had become very involved across a number of projects in the business and also developed his own interests and this indicated he was firmly embedded in the business environment. A1a finally accepted this.

A1a and A1b have an informal management structure for the business and this enables them to maintain responsibility over their areas whilst also encouraging creating diverse business opportunities. This has been particularly beneficial for A1b who developed business activities outside of the core family firms. In the first instance he set up a gift shop with his fiancé and a temporary seasonal shop with his sister on a short-term lease.

The relationship between A1a and A1b has improved considerably as they spent more time working together. A1b described how previously if he had personal problems he would share them with his sisters, however he subsequently had developed a closer rapport with his father. A1b also acknowledged that his father was more lenient with him than with other family members in a personal context and this was sometimes difficult for the others to understand. At the same time both father and son ensured that A1b's mother did not feel excluded as she felt she was the primary support mechanism for her son. In order to protect her feelings A1a and A1b did not allow family members to see how close they were by restricting personal conversations to the workplace.

The longer-term aspirations of father and son are to achieve growth in the business, however both generations have different ways of viewing this. A1a wants to identify new business opportunities that may provide a stronger base for development. A1b however feels that the current business can be developed and expanded to achieve this. Their compromise in this has been for A1b to lead on new projects under the current business with A1a adopting a more advisory role. Despite his initial reservations about A1b remaining in the business, A1a is keen to maintain a family firm that is managed and controlled internally.

Case A2

	A2	
Industry	Gas station and fast food franchise	
Year established	1987	
Founder	A2a	
Employee size	20 full-time and additional part-time	

	A2a	A2b
Relationship	Father	Son
Age	45–54	25–34
Business position	Director	Manager
Year of entry	1987	2003
Educational qualifications	Degree	Degree
Previous employment	✓	✓

A2a had previous experience of running business whilst in India. The business was not particularly successful and in his search for better opportunities his friends encouraged him to think about moving to America. With their encouragement he moved with his wife and baby son to California. Once there he got a job as a bank clerk where he worked for five years before being promoted to Vice President. At this stage he felt his employment prospects had climaxed as he would not have the opportunity to progress beyond that position. In the meantime his father was also encouraging him to think about starting up his own business. A2a and his wife set up a convenience store in partnership with A2a's brothers who were still working in the bank. A2a and his wife were responsible for managing the business, which they did for four years before deciding to sell their shares and consider alternative business opportunities. Part of the reason for this was the two-hour commute from their home to the business. A2a bought a number of retail units where he built up the business and sold on in order to make a bigger purchase. This enabled A2a and his family to move to Atlanta where he and his younger brother bought a discount dollar store. They opened a chain of seven units in this sector with the support of partners. However when the partners wanted to leave the business A2a and his brother could not afford to buy them out and so they sold the company. A2a then moved to Dallas and with his younger brother bought a petrol station and fast food franchise. He was able to establish the business by converting run-down stores into new franchises.

A2b had not expected to join the family business. After he graduated he worked as a financial analyst before moving into computing software. He was not very motivated working for someone else and did not feel the same monthly salary provided sufficient stimulus for working hard. He wanted to be in a position where his remuneration was directly linked to how hard he had worked. He was keen to join the family business but there was uncertainty on both sides. He started working in the business on an informal basis to get a feel for the experience and decided this was what he wanted to do and so resigned from his job. A2a was keen for A2b to develop his career in the professional field.

As a way of testing A2b's commitment he put him on probation in the company for three months and to work in a gas station as a trainee. On completion of his training A2b was very keen to remain in the business and his father was satisfied about this decision.

A2a and A2b have not always had a close personal relationship, largely due to A2a being in different states building up businesses whilst his children were growing up. Both father and son feel working together has enabled them to become closer, professionally and personally. They described their relationship as very good and open, they have different skills that complement each other. A2a acknowledges that his son generally listens to him and trusts his father's instinct. Both of their wives are involved in the daily management of the businesses. In addition they all live together as well. This creates a lot of crossover between home and work lives, business often dominates mealtime discussions. However, final decisions regarding the business are made between father and son.

The family do not have a retirement plan; however A2b feels that the business his father set up should support his parents in their retirement. Expansions that A2b is responsible provide benefit to him and his wife. The longer-term plans for the business are to achieve further growth with the possibility of diversification into other fields. Both generations are clear they want to maintain control of the business but enable more flexibility. A2b would like the opportunity to return to his career in order to update his skills and keep this as a viable option. A2a's plans for the business agree with this and possible options include retaining ownership but renting the businesses to external management.

Case A3

	A3	
Industry	Gas station and fast food franchise	
Year established	1998	
Founder	A3a	
Employee size	15 full-time + part-time	

	A3a	**A3b**
Relationship	Mother	Son
Age	55–64	25–34
Business position	President	Director
Year of entry	1992	1995
Educational qualifications	Degree	Junior year at University
Previous employment	✓	✓

This is an usual case compared to the others as A3a, the founder, is the mother. She previously worked as a secretary before resigning from her job having experienced discrimination under a new boss. Her initial experience of self-employment was a confectionery store she set up with her husband. The business did well and she gained greater confidence in her entrepreneurial abilities. A3a and her husband encouraged both of their children to get involved in the business from a young age and the extra manpower created opportunities for diversification. A3a set up other retail-based businesses that were built and sold on allowing a bigger investment each time. Finally A3a was able to get a foothold in the gas station market and build up a small chain of stations. The expansion occurred as a result of a partnership between A3a, her husband and an external partner.

A3b started studying marketing and finance at university, however he found he was not motivated to continue studying and so decided to take a year off. His initial plan had been to return to University, however having worked in a number of different companies he decided to remain in the business rather than return to University. His experience of working for other companies along with his experience of working in the family firm confirmed his desire to be self-employed. As his parents expanded their operations he became involved in the business and took over the running of one gas station. Over time this extended to the other stations in the company.

Although A3b's father has always been involved in the business the driving force behind the family is the mother. A3a and her son have a good working and personal relationship. Although A3a would have preferred her son to have completed his university education, she was also aware he came into the business at a critical time when it needed the manpower. In the meantime her daughter had been running the confectionery store but this was sold after her marriage.

Over time A3b was able to develop his own business interest. He diversified into the field of mortgages and set up his own company whilst working in the family firm. A3a, her husband and A3b have all developed their own areas of responsibility in the family business. This allows them to make decisions independently, however as they live together A3b feels there is a lot of crossover between their home and work life. A3a and A3b described how their domestic arrangements enable them to make decisions as a family, all three of them (including A3a's husband) sit down and discuss the merits of business decisions. Where there are differences of opinion, A3a and her husband will make the final decision.

Both generations had similar plans for the business although they were not well detailed. A3a wanted to continue expanding the business and ensuing it remained a family firm. A3b expected his mother to slowly withdraw from her senior position in order that he would increasingly take over responsibility. A3a made no mention of this. Their agreed plan was to remain in the same industry. A3b felt his parents were relying on him for their retirement and he was comfortable with this. No plans had been made regarding transition or succession.

References

Achua, C. 'Changing of the Old Guard for family businesses as "Boomers retire" and "Busters take over" ', *SBAER Conference Proceedings*, Florida (1997).

Adler, P. and Kwon, S. 'Social capital: Prospects for a new concept', *Academy of Management Review*, 27(1) (2002), 17–40.

Ahmed, A. *Bangladesh – Immigrant Entrepreneurs*, Unpublished DBA Thesis, Henley Management College (1981).

Akumu, J. 'Asians are their own worst enemy', *The Economic Review*, 3 June 1996, 30–32.

Aldrich, H., Cater, J., Jones, T. and McEvoy, D. 'Business development and self-segregation: Asian enterprise in three British cities' in C. Peach, V. Robinson and S. Smith (eds) *Ethnic Segregation in Cities* (London: Croom Helm, 1981).

Alibhai-Brown, Y. *Who Do We Think We Are? Imagining the New Britain* (London: Allen Lane/The Penguin Press, 2000).

Allen, S. *New Minorities, Old Conflicts: Asian and West Indian Immigrants in Britain* (New York: Random House, 1971).

Anwar, M. *The Myth of Return: Pakistanis in Britain* (London: Heinemann Education, 1977).

Arnold, F., Minocha, U. and Fawcett, J. T. 'The changing face of Asian immigration to the United States' in J.T. Fawcett and B.V. Carino (eds) *Pacific Bridges: The New Immigration from Asia and the Pacific Islands* (New York: Centre for Migration Studies, 1987).

Astrachan, J. H. 'Family firm and community culture', *Family Business Review* 1(2) (1988), 165–189.

Auster, E. and Aldrich, H. 'Small business vulnerability, ethnic enclaves and ethnic enterprise' in R. Ward and R. Jenkins (eds) *Ethnic Communities in Business* (Cambridge: Cambridge University Press, 1984).

Baines, S. and Wheelock, J. 'Working for each other: Gender, the household and micro-business survival and growth', *International Small Business Journal*, 17(1) (1998), 16.

Ballard, R. and Ballard, C. 'The Sikhs: The development of the South Asian settlements in Britain' in J. Watson (ed.) *Between Two Cultures: Migrants and Minorities in Britain* (Oxford: Basil Blackwell, 1984).

Ballard, R. and Hurst, C. (eds) *Desh Pardesh: The South Asian Presence in Britain* (London: Hurst Publishers, 1994).

Banks, M. *Ethnicity: Anthropological Constructs* (London: Routledge, 1996).

Basu, A. 'Asian small businesses in Britain: An exploration of entrepreneurial activity', Paper presented to the *Second International Journal of Entrepreneurial Behaviour and Research Conference*, Malvern (1995).

Basu, A. 'The role of institutionalised support in Asian entrepreneurial expansion in Britain', *Journal of Small Business & Enterprise Development* 5(4) (1999), 317–326.

Basu, A. 'Family and business: A study of Asian entrepreneurs in Britain', *The Family Business Network 11ᵗʰ Annual World Conference* (London: Academic Research Forum Proceedings, 2000).

Bates, T. 'Financing small business creation: The case of Chinese and Korean immigrant entrepreneurs', *Journal of Business Venturing* 12 (1997), 109–124.

Bates, T. *Race, Self-employment and Upward Mobility: An Elusive American Dream* (Netherlands: Kluwer Academic Publishers, 1999).

Bewayo, E. 'The Family and entrepreneurship in Uganda', *SBAER Conference Proceedings*, Florida, www.sbaer.uca.edu. (1997).

Bhushan, K. *Kenya 1997–1998, Factbook*, 15th edition (Nairobi: Newspread International, 1998).

Biers, D. and Dhume, S. 'In India, a bit of California', *Far Eastern Economic Review* 163(44) (2000), 38–41.

Birley, S. 'The start-up' in P. Burns and J. Dewhurst (eds) *Small Business and Entrepreneurship*, 2nd edition (Basingstoke: Macmillan, 1996).

Bjerke, B. 'Some inadequacies of Western models in understanding Southeast Asian entrepreneurship and SMEs', The 1998 ICSB Singapore Conference Proceedings, www.sbaer.uca.edu/Research/1998/ICSB (1998).

Boissevain, J., Blaschke, J., Grotenbreg, H., Joseph, I., Light, I., Sway, M., Waldinger, R. and Werbner, P. 'Ethnic entrepreneurs and ethnic strategies' in Waldinger *et al.* (eds) *Ethnic Entrepreneurs* (London: Sage Publications, 1990).

Bolton, J. *Small Firms: Report of the Committee of Inquiry on Small Firms* (London: HMSO, 1971).

Bonacich, E. and Modell, J. *The Economic Basis of Ethnic Solidarity: Small Business in the Japanese American Community* (Berkley: University of California, 1980).

Bourdieu, P. 'The forms of capital' in J.G. Richardson (ed.) *Handbook of Theory and Research for the Sociology of Education* (New York: Greenwood, 1985).

Bristow, M., Adam, B. and Pereira, C. 'Ugandan Asians in Britain, Canada and India: Some characteristics and resources', *New Community*, 5(2) (1975), 155–166.

Brockhaus, R. 'The psychology of the entrepreneur' in C. Kent, D. Sexton and K. Vesper (eds) *Encyclopedia of Entrepreneurship* (New Jersey: Prentice Hall, 1982).

Brockhaus, R. 'Family business succession: suggestion for future research', *Family Business Review*, 17(2) (2004), 165–178.

Butler, J. 'Review of *race, self-employment and upward mobility: An elusive American Dream*', *Small Business Economics*, 12(2) (1999), 183–188.

Butler, J. S. *Entrepreneurship and Self-help among Black Americans: A Reconsideration of Race & Economics* (United States: Transaction Publishers, 1991).

Butler, J. S. and Herring, C. 'Ethnicity and entrepreneurship', *Sociological Perspectives*, 34(1) (1991), 79–94.

Butler, J. E., Brown, B. and Chamornmarn, W. 'Informal networks, entrepreneurial action and performance', *Asia Pacific Journal of Management* 20(2) (2003), 151.

Butler-Cole, N. 'Succession and success', *Management Today*, May (1975), 52–56.

Caird, S. 'What does it mean to be enterprising?' *British Journal of Management*, 1(3) (1990), 137–145.

Carland, J. W., Hoy, F., Boulton, W. R. and Carland, J. A. C. 'Differentiating entrepreneurs from small business owners: A conceptualisation', *The Academy of Management Review*, 9(2) (1984), 354–359.

References 141

Carsud, A., Lara, S. and Sachs, R. 'Exploring a classification scheme for closely-held businesses: Getting to workable definitions of family firms', Paper presented at *The United States Association for Small Businesses & Entrepreneurship National Conference*, San Francisco (1997).

Castles, S. and Kosack, G. *Immigrant Workers and Class Structure in Western Europe*, 2nd edition (New York: Oxford University Press, 1985).

Chabria, A. 'Silicon Raj', *Upside* (US edition), 12(7) (2000), 148–154.

Chan, S. and Janjuha-Jivraj, S. 'Successional issues in ethnic family businesses: Blessing or burden?' Paper presented at *The Small Business & Enterprise Development Conference*, Manchester (2000).

Chandra, V. P. 'Remigration: Return of the prodigals – An analysis of the impact of the cycles of migration and remigration on caste mobility', *The International Migration Review*, 13(1) (1997), 162–170.

Chell, E. 'The social construction of the entrepreneurial personality', Paper presented at the British Academy of Management Conference, London (1997).

Chell, E., Haworth, J. and Brearley, S. *The Entrepreneurial Personality: Concepts, Cases and Categories* (London: Routledge, 1991).

Clark, D. 'South Asian "Angels" reap riches, spread wealth in Silicon Valley', *Wall Street Journal* (Eastern edition), New York, 2 May 2000.

Coleman, J. 'The rational reconstruction of society' (1992 Presidential Address) *American Sociological Review*, 58 (1993), 1–15.

Coser, L. *The Functions of Social Conflict* (London: Routledge and Kegan Paul Ltd, 1968).

Cramton, C. D. 'Is rugged individualism the whole story? Public and private accounts of a firm's founding', *Family Business Review*, 6(3) (1993), 233–261.

Curran, J. and Burrows, C. 'Ethnicity and enterprise: A national profile', Paper presented at the *11th National Small Firms Research and Policy Conference*, Cardiff (1988).

Curran, J., Jarvis, R., Blackburn, R. and Black, S. 'Networks and small firms', *International Small Business Journal*, 11(2) (1993), 13–25.

Daily, C. M. and Dollinger, M. J. 'Family firms are different', *Review of Business*, 13(1/2) (1991), 3–5.

Deakins, D., Majmuder, M. and Paddison, A. 'Enterprising futures: Success factors for ethnic minorities in business', Paper presented at *19th National Small Firms Research and Policy Conference*, Birmingham (1996).

Dhaliwal, S. *Silent Contributors – Asian Female Entrepreneurship and Women in Business* (London: Roehampton Institute, 1998).

Dumas, C. 'Understanding of father–daughter and father–son dyads in family-owned businesses', *Family Business Review*, 2(1) (1989), 31–46.

Dumas, C. 'Integrating the daughter into family business management', *Entrepreneurship, Theory and Practice*, 16(4) (1992), 41–46.

Durkheim, E. *The Division of Labour in Society* (New York: Free Press, 1984).

Dyck, B., Mauws, M., Mischke, G. and Starke, F. 'When father and son drop the succession baton: Toward a theory of executive succession', *SBAER Conference Proceedings*, San Diego, 14–17 January, www.sbaer.uca.edu. (1999).

Dyer, W. G. *Cultural Change in Family Firms: Anticipating and Managing Business and Family Traditions* (San Francisco: Jossey-Bass, 1986).

Dyer, W. G. 'Culture and community in family firms', *Family Business Review*, 1(1) (1988), 37–50.

Dyer Jr, W. G. and Handler, W. 'Entrepreneurship and family business: Exploring the connections', *Entrepreneurship, Theory and Practice*, 19(1) (1994), 71–83.

Enz, C. A., Dollinger, M. J. and Daily, C.M. 'The value orientations of minority and non-minority owned small business owners', *Entrepreneurship: Theory and Practice*, 15(1) (1990), 23–35.

Fairlie, R. *Self-employed Business Ownership Rates in the United States, 1979–2003, Small Business Research Summary*, Small Business Administration, No. 243, December (2004).

Ferrand, D. 'A study of the missing middle in Kenya', Paper presented at the *Institute for Development Studies Seminar*, Nairobi University (1996).

Finch, J. *Family Obligations and Social Change* (Oxford: Polity Press, 1989).

Fournier, V. and Lightfoot, G. 'Identity, work and family business', Paper presented at the *19th National Small Firms Research & Policy Conference*, Birmingham (1996).

Gerber, M. E. *The E-Myth Revisited* (New York: HarperCollins, 1995).

Gibb, A. 'Towards the building of entrepreneurial models of support for small business', Paper presented at the *11th National Small Firms Policy and Research Conference*, Cardiff (1988).

Gold, S. 'Gender and social capital among Israeli immigrants in Los Angeles', *Diaspora*, 4(267) (1995), 301.

Goodwin, R. and Cramer, D. *Social Support & Marital Well-being in an Asian Community*, Social Policy Research Paper No. 128 (1997).

Gray, K., Cooley, W. and Lutabingwa, J. 'Small scale manufacturing in Kenya', *Journal of Small Business Management*, 35(1) (1997), 66–72.

Greene, P. 'A resource-based approach to ethnic business sponsorship: A consideration of Ismaili-Pakistani immigrants', *Journal of Small Business Management*, 35(4) (1997), 58–72.

Handler, W. and Kram, K. 'Succession in family firms – the problem of resistance', *Family Business Review*, 1(4) (1988), 361–381.

Hill, M. F. *Permanent Way* (Nairobi: E. A. Railways and Harbours, 1949).

Himbara, D. *Kenyan Capitalists, the State and Development* (Nairobi: East African Educational Publishers, 1994).

Hiro, D. *Black British, White British – A History of Race Relations in Britain* (London: Grafton Books, 1991).

Ibrahim, G. and Galt, V. 'Ethnic business development: Toward a theoretical synthesis and policy framework', *Journal of Economic Issues*, 37(4) (2003), 1107.

Iganski, P. and Payne, G. 'Declining racial disadvantage in the British labour market', *Ethnic & Racial Studies*, 9(1) (1996), 113–134.

Janjuha-Jivraj, S. and Mansukhani, S. 'Daughters, the new breed of successors? A comparative study of Asian family businesses', Paper presented at the *25th National Small Firms Policy and Research Conference*, Brighton (2002).

Janjuha-Jivraj, S. 'The sustainability of social capital within ethnic networks', *Journal of Business Ethics*, 47 (2003), 31–43.

Janjuha-Jivraj, S. 'Social capital as a long-term resource among ethnic networks: The South Asian business community in Britain' in L. J. Spence, A. Habisch and R. Schmidpeter (eds) *Responsibility and Social Capital, The World of Small and Medium Sized Enterprises* (Basingstoke: Palgrave Macmillan, 2004a).

Janjuha-Jivraj, S. 'The impact of the mother during family business succession: Examples from the Asian business community', *Journal of Ethnic and Migration Studies*, 30(4) (2004b), 781–797.

Janjuha-Jivraj, S. and Woods, A. 'Successional issues within Asian family firms, learning from the Kenyan experience', *International Small Business Journal*, 20(1) (2001), 77–94.

Jones, G. and Rose, M. 'Family capitalism', *Business History*, 35(4) (1993), 1–43.

Jones, T., McEvoy, D. and Barrett, G. 'Labour intensive practices in the ethnic minority firm' in J. Atkinson and D. Storey (eds) *Employment, the Small Firm and the Labour Market* (London: Routledge, 1993).

Kanjanapan, W. 'The immigration of Asian professionals to the United States, 1988–1990', *International Migration Review*, 29(7) (1996), 7–32.

Kasarda, J.D. 'Urban industrial transition and the underclass', *The Annals of the American Academy*, 501 (1989), 26–47.

Kay, R. and Heck, Z. 'A commentary on "entrepreneurship in family vs. non-family firms: A resource based analysis of the effect on organisational culture" ', *Entrepreneurship: Theory and Practice*, 28(4) (2004), 383–390.

Kets de Vries, M. 'The entrepreneurial personality: A person at the crossroads', *Journal of Management Studies*, February, 14(1) (1977), 34–57.

Kets de Vries, M. 'The dynamics of family controlled firms: The good and the bad news', *Organizational Dynamics*, Winter 21(3) (1993), 59–72.

Kets de Vries, M. *Family Business: Human Dilemmas in the Family Firm* (London: International Thompson Business Press, 1996).

Khan, G. 'Size and growth of Asian-owned incorporated companies in Britain', *International Small Business Journal*, 7(1) (1988), 10–28.

Kloosterman, R. 'Immigrant entrepreneurship and the institutional context: A theoretical exploration' in J. Rath (ed.) *Immigrant Businesses: The Economic, Political and Social Environment* (Basingstoke: Palgrave Macmillan, 2000).

Kloosterman, R., Van der Leun, J. and Rath, J. 'Mixed embeddedness: (In)formal economic activity and immigrant businesses in the Netherlands', *International Journal of Urban Regional Research*, 23(2) (1999), 252.

Kuratko, D. 'Understanding the succession challenge in family businesses', *Entrepreneurship, Innovation and Change*, 4(3) (1995), 185–190.

Labour Force Survey (2002/03) 'Employment patterns', Published by Office for National Statistics, www.statistics.gov.uk (2005).

Landa, J. T. 'Underground economies: Generic or sui generic' in J. Jenkins (ed.) *Beyond the Informal Sector* (San Francisco: ICS Press, 1998).

Layton-Henry, Z. *The Politics of Immigration* (Oxford: Blackwell Publishers, 1992).

Le, C. N. 'A closer look at Asian Americans and education', *New Horizons for Learning*, September (2001), www.newhorizons.org.

Levenstein, M. 'African American entrepreneurship: The view from the 1910 Census', *Business and Economic History*, 24(1) (1995), 106–122.

Levinson, H. 'Conflicts that plague family businesses', *Harvard Business Review*, 1(2) (1971), 119–133.

Light, I. *Ethnic Enterprise in America: Business and Welfare among Chinese, Japanese and Blacks* (Berkley: University of California Press, 1972).

Light, I. 'Immigrant and ethnic enterprise in North America', *Ethnic and Racial Studies*, 7 (1984), 195–216.

Light, I. and Bonacich, E. *Immigrant Entrepreneurs: Koreans in Los Angeles, 1965–1982* (Berkeley, CA: University of California Press, 1988).

Luthra, M. *Britain's Black Population* (Oxford: Blackwell Publishers, 1997).

Marger, M. 'Social and human capital in immigrant adaptation: The case of Canadian business immigrants', *The Journal of Social Economics*, 30(2) (2001), 169.

Marger, M. N. and Hoffman, C. A. 'Ethnic entrepreneurship in Ontario: Immigrant participation in the small business sector', *International Migration Review*, 26(3) (1992), 968–981.

Mars, G. and Ward, R. 'Ethnic business development in Britain: Opportunities and resources' in R. Ward and R. Jenkins (eds) *Ethnic Communities in Business – Strategies for Economic Survival* (Cambridge: Cambridge University Press, 1984).

Marshack, K. J. 'Copreneurs and dual-career couples: Are they different?', *Entrepreneurship, Theory and Practice*, 19(1) (1994), 49–69.

Martin, C. *Accountancy Practices and the Provision of Ownership Succession Advice*, Research report no. 85, ACCA, Certified Accountants Educational Trust, London (2005).

Maslow, A. 'A theory of human motivation', *Psychological Review*, 50 (1943), 370–396.

Mattausch, J. 'From subjects to citizens: British East African Asians', *Journal of Ethnic & Migratory Studies*, 24(1) (1998), 121–141.

Matthews, C. and Moser, S. 'The impact of family background and gender on interest in small firms', Paper presented at the *Babson Kauffman Entrepreneurial Conference*, Ghent (1998).

McClelland, D. *The Achieving Society* (New Jersey: D.Van Nostrand Co. Inc., 1961).

Metcalf, H., Modood, T. and Virdee, S. *Asian Self-employment: The Interaction of Culture and Economies in England* (London: Policy Studies Institute, 1996).

Modood, T. *Not Easy Being British: Colour, Culture & Citizenship* (Stoke-on-Trent: Runneymede Trust & Trentham Books, 1992).

Modood, T. and Berthoud, R. *Ethnic Minorities in Britain: Diversity and Disadvantage* (London: Policy Studies Institute, 1997).

Moss Kanter, R. *The Change Masters* (London: Allen & Unwin, 1983).

Noah, T. 'Asian Americans take lead in starting US businesses – They often leave white-collar jobs in Asia for promise of more money', *Wall Street Journal*, 2 August 1991, 2.

Omwoyo, S. 'Introduction', *The East African Journal of History and Social Sciences*, 1(1) (1996), 1–6.

Owen, A. J. and Rowe, B. R. 'The cultural underpinnings of running family-owned firms', *Family Business Annual*, 1(1) (1995), 133–149.

Park, R. and Burgess, E. *Introduction to the Science of Sociology* (Chicago: University of Chicago Press, 1921).

Patel, Z. *Challenge to Colonialism* (Nairobi: Modern Lithographic (K) Limited, 1997).

Peach, C. *Ethnicity in the 1991 Census – Volume Two, The Ethnic Minority Populations of Britain* (London: HMSO, 1996).

Phizaclea, A. and Ram, M. 'Open for business? Ethnic entrepreneurship in comparative perspective', *Work, Employment and Society*, 10(2) (1996), 319–339.

Portes, A. 'Modes of structural incorporation and present theories of immigration' in M. Kritz, C. Keely and S. Tomasi (eds) *Global Trends in Migration* (Staten Island, NY: CMS Press, 1981).

Portes, A. 'Social capital: Its origins and applications in modern sociology', *Annual Review of Sociology*, 24(1) (1998), 1–25.

Portes, A. and Bach, R. *Latin Journey: Cuban and Mexican Immigrants in the United States* (California: University of California Press, 1985).

Poutziouris, P. and Chittenden, F. *Family businesses or business families?*, Institute for Small Business Affairs, Research Series, Monograph 1 (1996).

Rafiq, M. *Are Asians Taking over British Retailing?* Loughborough University, Research Paper 12 (1990).

Ram, M. *Managing to Survive – Working Lives in Small Firms* (Oxford: Blackwell, 1994).

Ram, M. and Hillin, G. 'Achieving break-out developing mainstream ethnic minority business', *Small Business Enterprise Development Journal*, 1 (1994), 15–21.

Ram, M. and Holliday, R. 'Keeping it in the family: Family culture in small firms' in F. Chittenden, M. Robertson and D. Watkins (eds) *Small Firms Recession and Recovery* (London: Paul Chapman Publishing, 1993).

Ram, M. and Jones, T. *Ethnic Minorities in Business*, Small Business Research Trust (Milton Keynes: Open University Business School, 1998).

Ram, M. and Smallbone, D. *Ethnic Minority Enterprise: Policy in Practice* (Sheffield: Small Business Service, 2001).

Ramdin, R. *The Making of the Black Working Class in Britain* (Aldershot: Gower, Wildwood House, 1987).

Rath, J. (ed.) *Immigrant Businesses: The Economic, Political and Social Environment* (New York: Palgrave Macmillan, 2000).

Reeves, T. J. and Bennett, C. E. *We the People: Asians in the United States Census 2000 Special Report*, US Department of Commerce (2004).

Reid, R., Dunn, B., Cromie, S. and Adams, J. 'Family orientation in family firms: A model and some empirical evidence', *Journal of Small Business and Enterprise Development*, 6(1) (1999), 55–67.

Rosenblatt, P., de Mik, L., Anderson, R. and Johnson, P. *The Family in Business: Understanding and Dealing with the Challenges Entrepreneurial Families Face* (San Francisco: Jossey-Bass, 1985).

Sanders, J. and Nee, V. 'Limits of ethnic solidarity in the enclave economy', *American Sociological Review*, 52 (1987), 745–773.

Saxenian, A. *Regional Advantage: Silicon Valley and Route 128*, 2nd edition (Oxford: Oxford University Press, 1998).

Saxenian, A. 'Silicon Valley's new immigrant high-growth entrepreneurs', *Economic Development Quarterly*, 16(1) (2002), 20–31.

Schumpeter, J. *The Theory of Economic Development*, translated by R. Opie from the second German edition [1926] (Cambridge: Harvard University Press, 1934).

Seidenberg, D. A. *Mercantile Adventurers: The World of East African Asians, 1750–1985* (New Delhi: New Age International (P) Ltd Publishers, 1996).

Shanker, M. and Astrachan, J. 'Myths and realities: Family business' contribution to the US economy', *SBAER Conference Proceedings*, www.sbaer.uca.edu./docs/proceedings/96usa021.txt (1996).

Sharma, P. 'An overview of the field of family business studies: Current status and directions for the future', *Family Business Review*, 17(1) (2004), 1–36.

Sharma, P., Chrisman, J. and Chua, J. 'An evaluation of family firm research from a Strategic Management Perspective', *Proceedings of United States Association for Small Business and Entrepreneurship* (1996), 33–42.

Sites, P. 'Needs as analogues of emotions' in J. Burton (ed.) *Conflict: Human Needs Theory: The Conflict Series* (USA: Macmillan, 1990).

Smith, S. 'Fortune and failure: The survival of family firms in eighteenth century India', *Business History*, 35(4) (1993), 44–65.

Soar, S. *Business Development Strategies, TECs and Ethnic Minorities Conference Report*, Home Office Ethnic Minority Business Initiative (1991).

Song, M. *Helping Out – Children's Labour in Ethnic Businesses* (Philadelphia: Temple University Press, 1999).

Spring, A. 'Gender and the range of African entrepreneurial strategies: The typical and the new woman entrepreneur' in A. Jalloh and T. Falola (eds) *African and African American Business: Historical and Contemporary Perspectives* (Rochester: University of Rochester Press, 2002).

Srinivasan, S. 'The class position of the Asian petty bourgeoisie', *New Community*, 19(1) (1992), 61–74.

Stanworth, J. and Gray, C. (eds) *Bolton 20 Years On: The Small Firms in the 1990s* (London: Paul Chapman Publishing on behalf of the Small Business Research Trust, 1991).

Stanworth, J., Stanworth, C., Granger, B. and Blyth, S. 'Who becomes an entrepreneur?', *International Small Business Journal*, 8(1) (1989), 11–22.

Stewart, A. 'Help one another, use one another: Toward an anthropology of family buisness', *Entrepreneurship: Theory and Practice*, 27(4) (2003), 383–397.

Strategy Unit, *Ethnic Minorities and the Labour Market*, Cabinet Office Report, March (2003).

Taiguri, R. and Davis, J. 'Bivalent attributes of the family firm', Working Paper, Harvard Business School, Cambridge, Mass. (1982), Reprinted *Family Business Review*.

Thompson, M. 'The second generation – Punjabi or English?', *New Community*, 3(3) (1974), 242–248.

Tinker, H. *The Banyan Tree: Overseas Emigrants from India, Pakistan and Bangladesh* (Oxford: Oxford University Press, 1977).

Waldinger, R., Aldrich, H. and Ward, R. (eds) *Ethnic Entrepreneurs* (London: Sage Publications, 1990).

Ward, J. L. *Keeping the Family Business Healthy* (San Francisco: Jossey Bass, 1987).

Ward, R. and Jenkins, R. *Ethnic Communities in Business – Strategies for Economic Survival* (Cambridge: Cambridge University Press, 1984).

Watson, J. (ed.) *Between Two Cultures: Migrants & Minorities in Britain* (Oxford: Basil Blackwell, 1984).

Weber, M. [1922] (1978) *Economy and Society* (Berkley and Los Angeles: University of California Press, cited in Sanders and Nee, 1987).

Werbner, P. 'Manchester Pakistanis: Life styles, ritual & the making of social distinction', *New Community*, 9 (1981), 216–229.

Werbner, P. 'Renewing an industrial past: British Pakistani entrepreneurship in Manchester', *Migration*, 8 (1990), 17–41.

Westhead, P. and Cowling, M. 'Family firm research: The need for a methodological rethink', *Entrepreneurship, Theory & Practice*, 23(1) (1998), 31–33.

Wheelock, J. and Oughton, E. 'The household as a focus for research', *Journal of Economic Issues*, 30(1) (1996), 143–150.

Wilson, A. *Family* (London: Tavistock Publications, 1985).

Wong, S. 'Business networks, cultural values and the state in Hong Kong and Singapore' in R. A. Brown (ed.) *Chinese Business Enterprise in Asia* (London: Routledge, 1995), 135–153.

Ybarra, M. J. 'International venture capitalists: India upside' (US edition) *Foster City*, 13(9) (2001), 42–50.

Zahra, S. A. and Sharma, P. 'Family business research: A strategic reflection', *Family Business Review*, 17(4) (2004), 331–346.

Index